DOES CAPITAL PUNISHMENT DETER CRIME?

Other books in the At Issue series:

DOES CAPITAL PUNISHMENT DETER CRIME?

Roman Espejo, *Book Editor*

Daniel Leone, *President*
Bonnie Szumski, *Publisher*
Scott Barbour, *Managing Editor*
Helen Cothran, *Senior Editor*

GREENHAVEN
PRESS®

San Diego • Detroit • New York • San Francisco • Cleveland
New Haven, Conn. • Waterville, Maine • London • Munich

For more information, contact
Greenhaven Press
27500 Drake Rd.
Farmington Hills, MI 48331-3535
Or you can visit our Internet site at http://www.gale.com

LIBRARY OF CONGRESS CATALOGING-IN-PUBLICATION DATA
Does capital punishment deter crime? / Roman Espejo, book editor.

    p. cm. — (At issue)
  Includes bibliographical references and index.
  ISBN 0-7377-1337-2 (pbk. : alk. paper) — ISBN 0-7377-1336-4 (lib. : alk. paper)
    1. Capital punishment—United States. 2. Punishment in crime deterrence—United States. I. Espejo, Roman, 1977– . II. At issue (San Diego, Calif.)
HV8699.U5 D645 2003
364.66—dc21   2002027156

Contents

Introduction

In March 2002, U.S. Attorney General John Ashcroft announced that the federal government would seek the death penalty for French-born Zacarias Moussaoui if he was found guilty of conspiracy charges related to the September 11, 2001, terrorist attacks on America. Moussaoui allegedly planned to join the team of hijackers that crashed airliners into the World Trade Center, the Pentagon, and a field in rural Pennsylvania. Ashcroft's announcement raised the question of whether capital punishment would deter future acts of terrorism.

Some commentators claim that executing Moussauoi would not deter, but provoke, retaliation from Islamic terrorists. Journalist Michelangelo Signorile argues that it would "only help ratchet up the culture of martyrdom where Islamic terrorism is rife, sending lots of teenage boys to their local terror camps to train for *jihad*," or holy war. However, others believe that using capital punishment would deter future terrorist acts because it would effectively incapacitate terrorists and send the clear message that terrorism is not tolerated. Bud Welch, a member of the board of directors for Murder Victims Families for Reconciliation, opposes the death penalty but states that "international terrorism is a different issue." He contends that if the United States apprehends the perpetrators of the September 11 attacks, it should execute them to stop future acts of terrorism on American soil.

The power of capital punishment to deter crime has been vigorously debated for decades. Over the years, researchers have attempted to add clarity to this debate by analyzing the relationship between executions and murder rates. In early twentieth-century studies, researchers comparatively examined the murder rates in states with and without capital punishment. Other experts compared murder rates for states before or after capital punishment was reintroduced or abolished. Researchers found that murder rates in states with and without capital punishment did not differ significantly. In addition, they found that murder rates did not decrease in states when capital punishment was reintroduced or increase when it was abolished.

However, later studies refuted these early findings. In the mid-1970s, after analyzing the national murder rate between 1930 and 1970, economist Isaac Ehrlich estimated that each execution prevents seven or eight murders. In a 2001 study, economists Hashem Dezhbakhsh, Paul Rubin, and Joana Mehlhop reported that each execution prevents between seven and twenty-five murders. Nonetheless, these more recent findings are also disputed. Statistics professor John Lambert argues that according to his analysis of the Ehrlich study, "the indication of deterrence was extremely unstable when small changes were made in Ehrlich's assumptions." In other words, Lambert believes that Ehrlich's findings cannot be reproduced consistently enough to support the claim that capital punishment deters crime. In regard to the 2001 study, the National Policy Committee (NPC) asserts that executions alone cannot account for the changes in the murder rate. The NPC claims that Dezhbakhsh, Rubin, and Mehlhop "also identified other factors that were associated with murder rates, including robbery and assault rates, per capita income in an area, and membership in the National Rifle Association."

The fact that so many studies have been conducted on the relationship between capital punishment and murder rates illustrates how central the issue of deterrence is in discussions about capital punishment. The theory of deterrence is based on the idea that criminal behavior can be deterred if punishment is swift, certain, and severe enough to counter the benefits or pleasure gained from committing crime. According to political science professors Silvia M. Mendes and Michael D. McDonald, "Deterrence theory holds that increasing the certainty of punishment, in the form of a higher probability of arrest and conviction, or increasing the severity of punishment . . . will raise the prospective costs of committing a crime. With a higher expected cost, crime is deterred." According to deterrence advocates, punishment deters crime in two ways. In "specific deterrence," convicted criminals are deterred from committing further crimes because they are physically unable to do so as a result of incarceration or execution. In "general deterrence," the threat of punishment deters other persons besides the convicted criminal from committing crimes.

Proponents believe that capital punishment deters crime more effectively than life imprisonment does. They point to its power of specific deterrence—executed criminals cannot kill or commit crime again. Political commentator James L. Sauer states that "any murderer who is executed will not murder again. Execution has a definite 'chilling' effect on repeaters. That cannot be said for . . . 'rehabilitation.'" Moreover, proponents argue that because of its severity, capital punishment is a more powerful form of general deterrence than is life imprisonment. Retired professor of jurisprudence Ernest van den Haag contends:

> The death penalty, because of its finality, is more feared than imprisonment, and deters some prospective murderers not deterred by the thought of imprisonment. Sparing the lives of even a few prospective victims by deterring their murderers is more important than preserving the lives of convicted criminals because of the possibility, or even the probability, that executing them would not deter others. . . . Penal sanctions are useful in the long run for the formation of the internal restraints so necessary to control crime. The severity and finality of the death penalty is appropriate to the seriousness and the finality of murder.

Numerous commentators claim that Texas, where approximately one-third of executions in the United States take place, has experienced a dramatic decline in its murder rate. Economics professor Morgan O. Reynolds claims that "the murder rate fell 60 percent since Texas started using the death penalty seriously in the 1990s, while the national murder rate fell 33 percent." Currently, Texas holds the record for the most executions in a single month and a single year—it executed twelve convicted murderers in April 1997 and forty in 2000.

Opponents of capital punishment, however, do not believe that capital punishment can be justified by the theory of general deterrence. They assert that most murders are impulsive acts committed by perpetrators who do not carefully consider or care about the consequences of their actions. Philosophy professor Hugo Adam Bedau insists that "most capital crimes are committed during moments of great emotional stress or under the influence of drugs or alcohol, when logical thinking has been suspended. Impulsive or expressive violence is inflicted by persons heedless of the consequences to themselves as well as to others." In addition, Bedau states that "the threat of even the severest punishment will not deter those who expect to escape detection and arrest."

Other critics of capital punishment suggest that capital punishment actually encourages murder and violent crime. They endorse the brutalization hypothesis—the idea that state-sanctioned executions send the message to individuals that killing one's enemies is justifiable. For example, after analyzing murder rates between 1907 and 1963 in the state of New York, researchers William J. Bowers and Glenn L. Pierce reported that there were an average of two additional homicides in the month after an execution. Also, another study alleges that four months after the highly publicized execution of convicted murderer Robert Alton Harris in 1992, the first person to be executed in California since 1967, the murder rate in California increased by 9 percent.

The deterrent effect of capital punishment is an important aspect of the capital punishment debate. Arguments for and against capital punishment's ability to deter murder and violent crime may be even more compelling after the September 11 terrorist attacks because of efforts to seek the death penalty for convicted terrorists. In *At Issue: Does Capital Punishment Deter Crime?* authors present divergent views on whether or not the most severe of punishments can deter the gravest crimes.

1

Capital Punishment Reduces Murder Rates

William Tucker

William Tucker is a writer living in Brooklyn, New York.

Although some studies indicate that states with capital punishment have historically higher rates of murder, a careful look at the statistics reveals that the enforcement of capital punishment deters—not increases—murder. Since 1994, states that have executed murderers have experienced the most rapid decline in homicide rates while states without capital punishment have seen an increase in murders. Therefore, the correlation between the higher numbers of executions and the higher murder rates reflects a state's decision to implement capital punishment in response to the seriousness of its murder problem.

Executing people for murder deters other people from committing other murders. Common sense would suggest to anyone that such a deterrent effect must exist. After all, people do fear losing their lives. And based on the evidence, it's hard to see why anyone would doubt the deterrent effect of the death penalty. Murder rates, which had trended downward since 1935, took off almost vertically after 1963, the year the Supreme Court started overturning state death penalty convictions on a routine basis. With capital punishment in abeyance, homicides rapidly climbed to unprecedented heights. From 4.9 per 100,000 in 1963, they doubled to 10.1 per 100,000 in 1972, two years after the Supreme Court finally overturned all existing capital punishment statutes. The national homicide rate reached a peak of 10.7 per 100,000 in 1980. And after a decade of dalliance when states condemned over 2,000 to death but executed only a handful, the rate was still at 10.5 per 100,000 in 1991.

By the beginning of the 1990s, however, states that wished to reimpose the ultimate penalty had fought their way through the endless thicket of appeals and restrictions imposed by the courts. In 1991, 14 murderers were executed while 2,500 waited on death row. By 1993 the figure had risen to 38 executions, then 55 in 1995, and 98 in 1999, a level not seen since the 1950s. (The all-time high of 200 executions occurred in 1935.) At the same time, murder rates began to plummet—to 9.6 per 100,000 in 1993, 7.7 in 1996, and 6.4 in 1999, the lowest level since 1966. To put the matter simply, over the past 40 years, homicides have gone up when executions have gone down and vice versa.

Does this constitute proof of deterrence? Not a chance, say the critics. There's no evidence of cause and effect. Dozens of other factors could explain these numbers. The decline might be just a coincidence.

The same, of course, can be said of all statistical correlations. All the potential factors must be separated out before anyone can draw conclusions. The only way to obtain proof would be to conduct a social experiment. (Retired professor of jurisprudence and public policy Ernest van den Haag, a supporter of the death penalty, once suggested executing people only for murders committed on Monday, Wednesday, and Friday, to see if there would be any migration of violent crime to other days of the week.) But such experiments would be completely unethical.

Death penalty regimes of the 50 states

The closest thing to this kind of experimentation that we have is the laboratory of the states—the differing death penalty regimes of the 50 states. And indeed, much attention has been lavished on the state-by-state figures, with the usual conclusion being that there is no deterrent effect from capital punishment, or even that executions may have a reverse effect. "Death-penalty states as a group do not have lower rates of criminal homicide than non-death-penalty states," says the American Civil Liberties Union (ACLU). "During the 1970s death-penalty states averaged an annual rate of 7.9 criminal homicides per 100,000 population; abolitionist states averaged a rate of 5.1."

In September 2000, the *New York Times* announced on the front page that its own survey had reached identical conclusions. "In a state-by-state analysis," said the report, "the *Times* found that during the last 20 years, the homicide rate in states with the death penalty has been 48 percent to 101 percent higher than in states without the death penalty. . . . Indeed, 10 of the 12 states without capital punishment have homicide rates below the national average, . . . while half the states with the death penalty have homicide rates above the national average . . . suggesting to many experts that the threat of the death penalty rarely deters criminals." Indeed, the figures might even support the allegations of some death penalty opponents that capital punishment *encourages* murder. After all, barbarity begets barbarity.

Executing people for murder deters other people from committing other murders.

The *Times* study is not as definitive as it may have appeared, however. It used figures only through 1996, even though 1998 numbers were available. (The ACLU, which lists execution-versus-murder-rate statistics on its website to prove "Capital Punishment is Not a Deterrent to Murder," stopped counting in 1995.) And the graph that accompanied the article seemed to show homicide rates falling a lot faster in states with capital punishment than without. Finally, the *Times* decided to leave New York and Kansas out of its survey, because these two states had adopted the death penalty only in the 1990s. New York's tumbling rate of crime would have had a considerable effect on the results obtained. But those are the choices involved in any survey.

An interesting pattern

The important thing is that, as crime statistics from the years subsequent to the ACLU and *New York Times* research have unfolded, a very interesting pattern has emerged: States with death penalties indeed started with historically higher rates of murder. But since 1994, murder rates in these states have fallen significantly, so that the gap between the two groups has been more than cut in half. If current trends continue, the divergence will disappear altogether.

This pattern can be seen most clearly if you put the states into three categories instead of the *Times*'s two: (1) states that execute people for murder; (2) states that have adopted a death penalty but have not executed anyone, and (3) states that have no death penalty. (This solves the problem of New York and Kansas, which fall neatly into the second category.) At the beginning of the decade, the three groups ranked in that order, top to bottom, in their rate of homicide. Murder rates in states that execute people were twice as high as in states without capital punishment, while states with capital punishment that have not yet executed anyone fell almost exactly in the middle. This would suggest that a state's decision on whether to adopt and implement capital punishment was influenced by how serious the problem of murder was perceived to be.

"The execution of each offender seems to save, on average, the lives of 18 potential victims."

Homicide rates have since fallen steadily in states that have performed executions, with the downward arc beginning in 1994. States with capital punishment but no executions have lowered their homicide rate but in a more uneven pattern. States with no capital punishment saw a slight decline that was almost completely wiped out by an upswing in 1999. Almost the entire drop in murder rates over the past decade has occurred in states with capital punishment, with the biggest decrease seen in states that are executing people.

States without capital punishment are generally liberal Democratic strongholds—Maine, Vermont, Massachusetts, Rhode Island, West Virginia, Michigan, Minnesota, Iowa, North Dakota, and Hawaii. Wisconsin and Alaska also have no death penalty. One feature that most share is a cold climate. "The best policeman in the world is a cold night" is an old law-enforcement adage, and states with severe winters have traditionally had lower crime rates. All of these states (except Michigan) also have relatively small African-American populations. Since African Americans commit murder at six times the rate of other population groups, this is likely to produce lower murder rates.

States with capital punishment that have not yet executed anyone tend to be states with liberal politics and large minority populations. New York, New Jersey, Connecticut, and New Mexico are representative. (The others are New Hampshire, Kansas, and South Dakota.) Combined, these states have only 27 people on death row and have not executed anyone. Often this is as much a reflection of jury decisions as state policies. In Connecticut, for example, a jury recently refused to impose the death penalty on a 25-year-old drug dealer, already serving a 35-year sentence, who had ordered the execution of a woman and her 8-year-old son because the boy had witnessed the murder of his mother's boyfriend, for which the drug dealer's brother was being tried. Although this heinous crime sparked a revision of the state's witness protection program, the jury did not see fit to impose the death penalty.

Capital punishment is a social policy that achieves targeted results.

Thirty-one states now have capital punishment and are performing executions. They are scattered across the map but tend to be concentrated in the South. Texas, Missouri, Oklahoma, Louisiana, Florida, Georgia, and Virginia have performed the majority of the nation's executions although Pennsylvania, Ohio, Montana, Idaho, Oregon, and Washington have had them as well. Generally these southern states have hot weather and large African-American populations, both of which have traditionally contributed to a higher murder rate.

Texas has had the highest number of executions (216 since 1990) and is constantly berated for it. Yet the results have been striking. In 1991, the state's murder rate was 15.3 per 100,000, second in the nation only to Louisiana. By 1999, it had fallen to 6.1, below 19 other states and close to the national average of 5.7. Florida (fourth in executions since 1990) has reduced its murder rate from 10.7 to 5.7. By contrast, non-executing New Mexico, with a similar climate and demographic profile, started the decade with a rate of 9.2 per 100,000 and ended with 9.8. Among the 31 states with executions, only four had a higher rate of murder at the end of the decade than at the beginning. Among the seven states with capital punishment but no executions, three finished with a higher rate of murder, while among the 12 states without capital punishment, five did.

Sophisticated and solid evidence

More sophisticated evidence of deterrence is also emerging. In 1976, Isaac Ehrlich, a University of Chicago researcher in econometrics, studied month-by-month patterns of murder and executions from data extending back into the 1930s. He found a deterrent effect of about eight murders for every execution. Ehrlich's study was introduced in evidence before the Supreme Court when it reversed its moratorium on executions in 1976, but the paper has since been subject to endless challenge and alleged refutation. In any case, the data are now outdated.

In May 2001, Hashem Dezhbakhsh, Paul Rubin, and Joanna Shepherd, three Emory University economists, published an updated version of Ehrlich's analysis using county-by-county data gathered since the renewal of executions. "Our results suggest the legal change allowing executions beginning in 1977 has been associated with significant reductions in homicide," they conclude. "In particular, the execution of each offender seems to save, on average, the lives of 18 potential victims." The authors estimate a margin of error of plus-or-minus 10, meaning as many as 28 but no less than 8 potential victims are saved with each execution.

This solid evidence of a deterrent effect should become a part of the death penalty debate. Whether it is wrong to execute people who are retarded, whether the indigent get sufficient legal counsel, whether African Americans are over- or underrepresented on death row, the role of DNA evidence in death-row cases—all these are questions to be debated on their merits. To date, however, opponents of the death penalty have all too often simply asserted that capital punishment has been proved to lack a deterrent effect. This of course means that defenders of the death penalty get cast as defenders of some barbaric ritual—as if they were in favor of sacrificing a virgin in the springtime in order to ensure a good harvest.

To the contrary, capital punishment is a social policy that achieves targeted results. Its very success is what now allows people to talk about some of its secondary aspects in a tranquil environment. With murders down nearly 40 percent since 1991, public alarm has abated. Those who would use this opportunity to abolish capital punishment must reckon with the innocent lives that will be lost if they succeed.

2

Capital Punishment Does Not Reduce Murder Rates

Raymond Bonner and Ford Fessenden

Raymond Bonner is a reporter for the New York Times *and author of* Waltzing with a Dictator: The Marcoses and the Making of American Policy. *Ford Fessenden is also a reporter for the* New York Times.

Capital punishment does not deter murder. FBI statistics reveal that ten of twelve states without capital punishment have murder rates below the national average. Furthermore, numerous experts believe that the presence or absence of capital punishment in a state is not a deciding factor in the actions of murderers.

The dozen states that have chosen not to enact the death penalty since the Supreme Court ruled in 1976 that it was constitutionally permissible have not had higher homicide rates than states with the death penalty, government statistics and a new survey by *The New York Times* show.

Indeed, 10 of the 12 states without capital punishment have homicide rates below the national average, Federal Bureau of Investigation data shows, while half the states with the death penalty have homicide rates above the national average. In a state-by-state analysis, *The Times* found that from 1980 to 2000, the homicide rate in states with the death penalty has been 48 percent to 101 percent higher than in states without the death penalty.

The study by *The Times* also found that homicide rates had risen and fallen along roughly symmetrical paths in the states with and without the death penalty, suggesting to many experts that the threat of the death penalty rarely deters criminals.

"It is difficult to make the case for any deterrent effect from these numbers," said Steven Messner, a criminologist at the State University of New York at Albany, who reviewed the analysis by *The Times*. "Whatever the factors are that affect change in homicide rates, they don't seem to operate differently based on the presence or absence of the death penalty in a state."

That is one of the arguments most frequently made against capital punishment in states without the death penalty—that and the assertion that it is difficult to mete out fairly. Opponents also maintain that it is too expensive to prosecute and that life without parole is a more efficient form of punishment.

Prosecutors and officials in states that have the death penalty are as passionate about the issue as their counterparts in states that do not have capital punishment. While they recognize that it is difficult to make the case for deterrence, they contend that there are powerful reasons to carry out executions. Rehabilitation is ineffective, they argue, and capital punishment is often the only penalty that matches the horrific nature of some crimes. Furthermore, they say, society has a right to retribution and the finality of an execution can bring closure for victims' families.

Polls show that these views are shared by a large number of Americans. And, certainly, most states have death penalty statutes. Twelve states have chosen otherwise, but their experiences have been largely overlooked in recent discussions about capital punishment.

A wise decision

"I think Michigan made a wise decision 150 years ago," said the state's governor, John Engler, a Republican. Michigan abolished the death penalty in 1846 and has resisted attempts to reinstate it. "We're pretty proud of the fact that we don't have the death penalty," Governor Engler said, adding that he opposed the death penalty on moral and pragmatic grounds.

Governor Engler said he was not swayed by polls that showed 60 percent of Michigan residents favored the death penalty. He said 100 percent would like not to pay taxes.

In addition to Michigan, and its Midwestern neighbors Iowa, Minnesota, North Dakota and Wisconsin, the states without the death penalty are Alaska, Hawaii, West Virginia, Rhode Island, Vermont, Maine and Massachusetts, where an effort to reinstate it was defeated in 1999.

No single factor explains why these states have chosen not to impose capital punishment. Culture and religion play a role, as well as political vagaries in each state. In West Virginia, for instance, the state's largest newspaper, *The Charleston Gazette*, supported a drive to abolish the death penalty there in 1965. Repeated efforts to reinstate the death penalty have been rebuffed by the legislature.

From 1980 to 2000, the homicide rate in states with the death penalty has been 48 percent to 101 percent higher than in states without the death penalty.

The arguments for and against the death penalty have not changed much. At Michigan's constitutional convention in 1961, the delegates heard arguments that the death penalty was not a deterrent, that those executed were usually the poor and disadvantaged, and that innocent people had been sentenced to death.

"The same arguments are being made today," said co-chairman of the

Michigan Committee Against Capital Punishment Eugene G. Wanger, who had introduced the language to enshrine a ban on capital punishment in Michigan's constitution at that convention. The delegates overwhelmingly adopted the ban, 141 to 3. Mr. Wanger said two-thirds of the delegates were Republicans, like himself, and most were conservative. In 1999, a former state police officer introduced legislation to reinstate the death penalty. He did not even get the support of the state police association, and the legislation died.

[In 1998] the homicide rate in North Dakota, which does not have the death penalty, was lower than the homicide rate in South Dakota, which does have it.

In Minnesota, which abolished capital punishment in 1911, 60 percent of the residents support the death penalty, said Susan Gaertner, a career prosecutor in St. Paul and the elected county attorney there since 1994. But public sentiment had not translated into legislative action, Ms. Gaertner said. "The public policy makers in Minnesota think the death penalty is not efficient, it is not a deterrent, it is a divisive form of punishment that we simply don't need," she said.

In Honolulu, the prosecuting attorney, Peter Carlisle, said he had changed his views about capital punishment, becoming an opponent, after looking at the crime statistics and finding a correlation between declines in general crimes and in the homicide rates. "When the smaller crimes go down—the quality of life crimes—then the murder rate goes down," Mr. Carlisle said.

Therefore, he said, it was preferable to spend the resources available to him prosecuting these general crimes. Prosecuting a capital case is "extremely expensive," he said.

Capital and noncapital cases

By the very nature of the gravity of the case, defense lawyers and prosecutors spend far more time on a capital case than a noncapital one. It takes longer to pick a jury, longer for the state to present its case and longer for the defense to put on its witnesses. There are also considerably greater expenses for expert witnesses, including psychologists and, these days, DNA experts. Then come the defendant's appeals, which can be considerable, but are not the biggest cost of the case, prosecutors say.

Mr. Carlisle said his views on the death penalty had not been affected by the case of Bryan K. Uyesugi, a Xerox copy machine repairman who gunned down seven co-workers in November 1999, in the worst mass murder in Hawaii's history. Mr. Uyesugi was convicted in June and is serving life without chance of parole.

Mr. Carlisle has doubts about whether the death penalty is a deterrent. "We haven't had the death penalty, but we have one of the lowest murder rates in the country," he said. The F.B.I.'s statistics for 1998, the last year for which the data is available, showed Hawaii's homicide rate was the fifth-lowest.

The homicide rate in North Dakota, which does not have the death penalty, was lower than the homicide rate in South Dakota, which does have it, according to F.B.I. statistics for 1998. Massachusetts, which abolished capital punishment in 1984, has a lower rate than Connecticut, which had six people on death row in 2000; the homicide rate in West Virginia is 30 percent below that of Virginia, which has one of the highest execution rates in the country.

Other factors affect homicide rates, of course, including unemployment and demographics, as well as the amount of money spent on police, prosecutors and prisons.

But the analysis by *The Times* found that the demographic profile of states with the death penalty is not far different from that of states without it. The poverty rate in states with the death penalty, as a whole, was 13.4 percent in 1990, compared with 11.4 percent in states without the death penalty.

Mr. Carlisle's predecessor in Honolulu, Keith M. Kaneshiro, agrees with him about deterrence. "I don't think there's a proven study that says it's a deterrent," Mr. Kaneshiro said. Still, he said, he believed that execution was warranted for some crimes, like a contract killing or the slaying of a police officer. Twice while he was prosecuting attorney, Mr. Kaneshiro got a legislator to introduce a limited death penalty bill, but, he said, they went nowhere.

"You don't solve violence by committing violence."

In general, Mr. Kaneshiro said, Hawaiians fear that the death penalty would be given disproportionately to racial minorities and the poor.

In Milwaukee, the district attorney since 1968, E. Michael McCann, shares the view that the death penalty is applied unfairly to minorities. "It is rare that a wealthy white man gets executed, if it happens at all," Mr. McCann said.

Those who "have labored long in the criminal justice system know, supported by a variety of studies and extensive personal experience, that blacks get the harsher hand in criminal justice and particularly in capital punishment cases," Mr. McCann wrote in "Opposing Capital Punishment: A Prosecutor's Perspective," published in the *Marquette Law Review* in 1996. Forty-three percent of the people on death row across the country are African-Americans, according to the National Association for the Advancement of Colored People (NAACP) Legal Defense and Educational Fund.

The death penalty also has been employed much more often when the victim was white—82 percent of the victims of death row inmates were white, while only 50 percent of all homicide victims were white.

Supporters of capital punishment who say that executions are justified by the heinous nature of some crimes often cite the case of Jeffrey L. Dahmer, the serial killer who murdered and dismembered at least 17 boys and men, and ate flesh from at least one of his victims.

Mr. McCann prosecuted Mr. Dahmer, but the case did not dissuade him from his convictions on the death penalty. "To participate in the

The Death Penalty and Homicide Rates

Homicide rates in states with the death penalty are higher than in those without, and have shown similar up-and-down trends over the years, offering little support to the contention that capital punishment is a deterrent.

Homicide Rate *per 100,000*

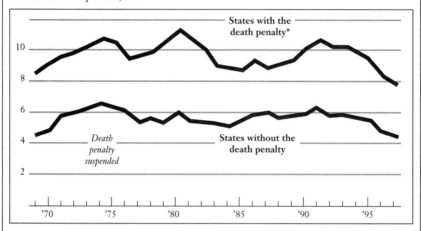

*Does not include New York or Kansas, which adopted the death penalty in the 1990s.

Source: Analysis by the *New York Times* (homicide rates).

killing of another human being, it diminishes the respect for life. Period," Mr. McCann said. He added, "Although I am a district attorney, I have a gut suspicion of the state wielding the power of the death over anybody."

Not a deterrent of any consequence

In Detroit, John O'Hair, the district attorney, similarly ponders the role of the state when looking at the death penalty.

Borrowing from Justice Louis E. Brandeis, Mr. O'Hair said: "Government is a teacher, for good or for bad, but government should set the example. I do not believe that government engaging in violence or retribution is the right example. You don't solve violence by committing violence."

Detroit has one of the highest homicide rates in the United States—five times more than New York in 1998—but Mr. O'Hair said bringing back the death penalty is not the answer.

"I do not think the death penalty is a deterrent of any consequence in preventing murders," said Mr. O'Hair, who has been a prosecutor and judge since 1970. Most homicides, he said, are "impulsive actions, crimes of passion," in which the killers do not consider the consequences of what they are doing.

Nor, apparently, do the people of Detroit see the death penalty as a way of cutting crime. Only 45 percent of Detroit residents favored capital punishment, a poll by EPIC/MRA, a polling organization in Lansing, Mich., found in 1999; in Michigan over all, 59 percent favored executions, which is roughly the level of support for the death penalty nationally.

"Life in prison without parole is about as punitive as you can get."

To illustrate the point that killers rarely considered the consequences of their actions, a prosecutor in Des Moines, John Sarcone, described the case of four people who murdered two elderly women. They killed one in Iowa, but drove the other one across the border to Missouri, a state that has the death penalty.

Mr. Sarcone said Iowa prosecutors were divided on the death penalty, and legislation to reinstate it was rejected by the Republican-controlled legislature in 1997. The big issue was cost, he said.

In 1999, in Michigan, Larry Julian, a Republican from a rural district, introduced legislation that would put the death penalty option to a referendum.

But Mr. Julian, a retired state police officer, had almost no political support for the bill, not even from the Michigan State Troopers Association, he said, and the bill died without a full vote. The Catholic Church lobbied against it.

State officials in Michigan are generally satisfied with the current law. "Our policies in Michigan have worked without the death penalty," said Matthew Davis, spokesman for the Michigan Department of Corrections. "Instituting it now may not be the most effective use of people's money."

Serving life without parole

In 2000, in Michigan, 2,572 inmates are serving sentences of life without parole, and they tend to cause fewer problems than the general prison population, Mr. Davis said.

They are generally quieter, not as insolent, more likely to obey the rules and less likely to try to escape, he said. Their motivation is quite clear, he said: to get into a lower security classification. When they come in, they are locked up 23 hours a day, 7 days a week, and fed through a small hole in the door. After a long period of good behavior, they can live in a larger cell, which is part of a larger, brighter room, eat with 250 other prisoners, and watch television.

One thing they cannot look forward to is getting out. In Michigan, life without parole means you stay in prison your entire natural life, not that you get out after 30 or 40 years, Mr. Davis said.

In many states, when life without parole is an option the public's support for the death penalty drops sharply. "The fact that we have life without parole takes a lot of impetus from people who would like to see the death penalty," said Ms. Gaertner, the chief prosecutor in St. Paul.

In most states with the death penalty, life without parole is not an option for juries. In Texas, prosecutors have successfully lobbied against legislation that would give juries the option of life without parole instead of the death penalty.

Mr. Davis said a desire "to extract a pound of flesh" was behind many of the arguments for capital punishment. "But that pound of flesh comes at a higher price than a lifetime of incarceration."

Mr. O'Hair, the Detroit prosecutor said, "If you're after retribution, vengeance, life in prison without parole is about as punitive as you can get."

3

Capital Punishment Saves Innocent Lives

Ernest van den Haag

Ernest van den Haag was a John M. Olin Professor of jurisprudence and public policy at Fordham University in New York City. He died in March 2002.

The sanction of capital punishment is needed to deter murder. Life sentences have less of a deterrent effect on murder than capital punishment because incarcerated murderers can escape, be released on furlough, or kill other prisoners or prison staff. Furthermore, arguments that capital punishment is counterproductive in the fight against crime are flawed. For instance, executions do not decrease the public's sensitivity to the immorality of murder and result in the increase of homicide or violent crime. Also, capital punishment is advantageous in murder prosecutions—it can be used to persuade accomplices to testify against murderers or elicit guilty pleas from murderers in exchange for a life sentence. Because it effectively saves the lives of innocent people, capital punishment must be enforced.

Suum cuique tribue (to give to everyone what he deserves) is to do justice. What is deserved? In penal justice this depends on the gravity of the crime and the culpability of the criminal, both hard to determine. There is no objective measure of the cardinal gravity of a crime; or of the cardinal severity of a punishment; nor, finally, do we have an objective indication of what punishment is deserved per se by each degree of gravity.

However, ordinal ranking is possible. Crimes of a similar kind can be arrayed according to comparative gravity; and punishments according to comparative severity. Although ultimately it depends on subjective evaluations too, ordinal ranking is helpful, e.g., by telling us that murder with torture, or with premeditation, (or multiple murder), is more grave (and deserves more punishment) than murder without—even if we cannot determine how much more. We can conjecture also that manslaughter deserves more punishment than assault, or theft, and menacing less. But we cannot determine how much more or less, nor whether execution is more severe than life in prison (most convicts think so).

Lex talionis

Physical punishments, such as mutilations, are more readily coordinated with the crimes they punish. Thus, the ancient *lex talionis*[1] required fewer decisions on the comparative gravity of harms and punishments. But the *lex talionis* is irrelevant to criminal justice. It treated crimes as torts, which entitled victims to retaliation or compensation according to the harm inflicted, whereas we consider crimes mainly as harms to society, which entitle it (and only it) to retribution. Retribution, as deserved by the crime, is the paramount moral purpose of punishment. It is an end in itself, a categorical imperative. Doing justice by retribution is an expressive, rather than an instrumental act, retrospective by definition. The very notion of "punishment" is retrospective.

Still, retributive punishment may yield legitimate, instrumental, nonmoral (though not immoral) benefits. Being instrumental, these benefits are prospective. Thus, incapacitation of the convict by imprisonment, while it lasts, obviously protects society. Rehabilitation (sometimes called specific deterrence) may help to protect society by discouraging crimes by the released convict. Deterrence, finally, restrains others than the convict from doing in the future what he did in the past. It is the most important instrumental benefit of punishment.

Deterrence is the only purpose of the threats of the criminal law.

Although a desirable effect consistent with it, deterrence is not part of the moral aim of justice. Deterrence can be justified, however, as an important instrumental purpose of punishment, if not as an independent one. It would be unjust to punish any person, guilty or innocent, merely to deter others. However, the deterrent effect of just (deserved) punishment, intended or not, is morally justifiable, since the convict volunteered for risking the punishment which has deterrent effects. He is not punished merely to deter others, which would be inconsistent with justice, even if he is guilty. However, if his deserved punishment deters others, it helps to repay for the harm the crime did to the social order—to pay his "debt to society."

Many abolitionists insist that the death penalty is no more deterrent than life in prison. This empirical question is, in principle, answerable by experiments, which, however, are seldom practical, feasible, or conclusive. But the justice of a punishment, such as the death penalty, as distinguished from deterrent effects, cannot be proved or disproved by any experiment. . . .

Deterrence is the only purpose of the threats of the criminal law. Punishment of those who were not deterred carries out these threats and 1) retributes, and 2) keeps the promise of the law (a threat is a negative promise and promises must be kept—*pacta sunt servanda*). So much for the moral purposes of punishment.

---

1. The law of retaliation. In the Hebrew scriptures, it is "an eye for an eye, a tooth for a tooth, an arm for an arm, a life for a life."

There are two non-moral (instrumental) purposes of punishment as well: 1) Legal threats of punishment would become incredible and lose their deterrent effectiveness if not carried out by actual punishment; and 2) the conditional threat of punishment addressed to prospective criminals is also a positive promise to the law abiding, which may help to keep them law abiding. If threats were not carried out against those not deterred by them, the law abiding, who took the threats seriously and formed the habit of abiding by the law, would have been fooled. At least some of them may have foregone crimes in part because they believed that they would be punished if they committed them. If those who were not deterred are not punished, the legal threats which helped restrain the law abiding would be revealed as bluffs. Criminals would have gained an advantage by breaking the law, while the law abiding would have been placed at a disadvantage by trusting the law. The social order which depends on the formation of law abiding habits would be undermined.

The most grave of crimes

Traditionally murder has been thought the most grave of crimes, deserving the most severe punishment. Other crimes, such as theft, or even rape, leave the victim capable of recovering. Murder does not. It is final. So is the death penalty, which, therefore, traditionally has been thought fitting.

The threat of capital punishment for murder is not counter-productive, whereas it might be for most other crimes.

Can any crime be horrible enough to forfeit the life of the criminal? Can death ever be a deserved punishment? Some abolitionists do not think so. Others even believe, for unintelligible reasons, that no society has a moral right to impose the death penalty. I am confident that the following excerpt may help answer this question. (*Res ipsa loquitur* [the thing speaks for itself].)

> . . . The appellant, after telling [seventeen-year-old] Donna Marie Dixon how pretty she was, raised his fist and hit her across the face. When she stood up, he grabbed her by her blouse, ripping it off. He then proceeded to remove her bra and tied her hands behind her back with a nylon stocking. Timothy McCorquodale then removed his belt, which was fastened with a rather large buckle, and repeatedly struck Donna across the back with the buckle end of the belt. He then took off all her clothing and then bound her mouth with tape and a washcloth. Leroy then kicked Donna and she fell to the floor. McCorquodale took his cigarette and burned the victim on the breasts, the thigh, and the navel. He then bit one of Donna's nipples and she began to bleed. He asked for a razorblade and then sliced the other nipple. He then called for a box of salt and poured it into the wounds he had made on her breasts. At this point Linda

[McCorquodale's girlfriend], who was eight months pregnant, became ill and went into the bedroom and closed the door. McCorquodale then lit a candle and proceeded to drip hot wax over Donna's body. He held the candle about 1/2 inch from Donna's vagina and dripped the hot wax into this part of her body. He then used a pair of surgical scissors to cut around the victim's clitoris.

While bleeding from her nose and vagina, Leroy forced the victim to perform oral sex on him while McCorquodale had intercourse with her. Then Leroy had intercourse with the victim while McCorquodale forced his penis into the victim's mouth. McCorquodale then found a hard plastic bottle which was about 5 inches in height and placed an antiseptic solution within it, forcing this bottle into Donna's vagina and squirted the solution into her. The victim was then permitted to go to the bathroom to "get cleaned up." While she was in the bathroom, McCorquodale secured a piece of nylon rope and told Bonnie and her roommate that he was going "to kill the girl." He hid in a closet across the hall from the bathroom and when Donna came out of the bathroom he wrapped the nylon cord around her neck. Donna screamed, "My God, you're killing me." As McCorquodale tried to strangle her, the cord cut into his hands and Donna fell to the floor. He fell on top of her and began to strangle her with his bare hands. He removed his hands and the victim began to have convulsions. He again strangled her and then pulled her head up and forward to break her neck. He covered her lifeless body with a sheet and departed the apartment to search for a means of transporting her body from the scene. By this time, it was approximately 6:00 A.M. on the morning of January 17, 1974.

McCorquodale soon returned to the apartment and asked Bonnie for her trunk and Leroy and McCorquodale tried to place Donna's body in the trunk. Finding that the body was too large for the trunk McCorquodale proceeded to break Donna's arms and legs by holding them upright while he stomped on them with his foot. Donna's body was then placed in the trunk and the trunk was placed in the closet behind the curtains. McCorquodale and Leroy then went to sleep on the couch in the living room for the greater portion of the day, leaving the apartment sometime during the afternoon.

Because a strong odor began to emanate from the body, and her efforts to mask the smell with deodorant spray had been unsuccessful, Linda called Bonnie to request that McCorquodale remove the trunk from the apartment. Shortly after 8:00 P.M. McCorquodale arrived at the apartment with a person named Larry. As they attempted to move the trunk from the closet, blood began spilling from the trunk onto the living room floor. McCorquodale placed a towel under the trunk to absorb the blood as they carried the trunk to Larry's car. When McCorquodale and Larry returned to the apartment they told Linda that the body had been dumped out of the trunk into a road and that the trunk was placed under some boxes in a "Dempsey Dumpster." Donna's body was found about half a mile off Highway No. 42 in Clayton County, Georgia. [McCorquodale was convicted of murder, and executed on September 21, 1987.]

The sanctity of life

Former Supreme Court Justice William Brennan thought the death penalty inconsistent with "the sanctity of life." His unargued notion may derive from the ancient *homo homini res sacra* (man is a sacred object to man). But the Romans, who coined the phrase, believed the sanctity of life best safeguarded by executing murderers who had not respected it. Brennan may also have based his view on the Constitution. However, it does not grant an imprescriptible right to life which murderers would be as entitled to as their victims. He also held that execution is a "denial of the executed person's humanity." Yet, philosophers, such as Immanuel Kant and G.W.F. Hegel, thought that punishments, including the death penalty, recognize and asseverate the humanity of the convict, even though he himself may have repudiated it by his crime.

We protect ourselves from ferocious beasts, but we do not punish them, because, unlike criminals, they cannot tell right from wrong or restrain themselves accordingly. Animals therefore are not, but criminals are responsible for their actions because they are human. Their punishment acknowledges rather than denies their responsibility and, thereby, their humanity. Brennan finally asserts that "the deliberate extinguishment of human life by the state is uniquely degrading to human dignity." He does not tell whether the criminal or the executioner is degraded, nor wherein the degradation lies, or whether any crime could degrade humanity and call for a degrading punishment.

The lifer may endanger guards and fellow prisoners, since without the death penalty there is no further punishment to deter him.

Capital punishment, a deliberate expulsion from human society, is meant to add deserved moral ignominy to death. This irks some abolitionists, who feel that nobody should be blamed for whatever he does. But murder deserves blame. Death may well be less punishment than what some criminals deserve. Even torture may be. But, although they may deserve it, we no longer torture criminals. Unlike death, torture is avoidable. It is now repulsive to most people, and no longer thought entertaining, as it was in the past.

However much deserved, the death penalty should not be imposed if, by not threatening it, we can save innocent lives. If (unlike the Supreme Court) we believe that rape deserves capital punishment, we nevertheless should not impose it because the threat would be an incentive to the rapist to murder his victim and make apprehension and conviction less likely without increasing the severity of his punishment if convicted. Indeed, capital punishment should be threatened rarely, because it would give threatened criminals—e.g. burglars—an incentive to kill victims, witnesses and arresting officers. However, the importance of trying to deter a first murder by the threat of capital punishment outweighs the usefulness of not encouraging additional murders by not threatening capital punishment for the first. Therefore, the threat of capital punishment for murder is not counter-productive, whereas it might be for most other crimes.

Abolitionists appear to believe that the non-execution of murderers is morally more important than saving the innocent lives execution would save if it deters more than imprisonment.

Nature has sentenced us all to death. Execution hastens, but does not create the unavoidable end of human life. What makes execution different is that it brands the executed as morally unworthy to belong to human society. The phrase "death is different," darkly intoned by abolitionists, is impressive and rings true, although it applies to execution more than to death. What follows from it? More capital punishment, or less? Or just caution in inflicting it?

Retributive justice

The paramount moral purpose of punishment is retributive justice. But there are important non-moral purposes as well, such as protection of life and property. They are achieved mainly by deterrence. It seems obvious that more severe and certain punishments deter more than less severe and certain ones. Yet, abolitionists contend that the death penalty is no more deterrent than life in prison, or, alternatively, that the additional deterrence is redundant. As mentioned, this empirical question could be decided by experiment. We could threaten capital punishment for murders committed on Mondays, Wednesdays, and Fridays (MWF) and life imprisonment on the other days. If fewer murders are committed on MWF, the death penalty would be likely to be more deterrent than life in prison. However, the MWF murders do not deserve more punishment than the others. It would be morally capricious to impose the death penalty just on MWF murderers. We will have to rely on observation and statistical analysis, rather than experiment, to establish degrees of deterrence. Preponderantly, though not conclusively, the data tend to show the death penalty to be the most deterrent punishment available. Possibly, people fear the death penalty irrationally, despite low probability (executions are rare), just as they are irrationally attracted to lotteries with high prizes despite the low probability of winning.

Apart from less deterrence, life imprisonment, the alternative to capital punishment, also protects society less than capital punishment does. The convict may escape, he may be granted a furlough, or his sentence may be commuted by governors who, unavoidably, retain the right to pardon. Not least, the lifer may endanger guards and fellow prisoners, since without the death penalty there is no further punishment to deter him.

To proponents of capital punishment, deterrence, though important, is not decisive. Justice is. Still, most believe that the threat of execution does deter more than life imprisonment. In contrast, abolitionists believe that capital punishment not only is morally unjustifiable, but also has no more deterrent effect than life imprisonment. However, they would continue to advocate abolition, even if the death penalty were shown to deter more than life imprisonment. In effect, abolitionists appear to believe that the non-execution of murderers is morally more important than saving the innocent lives execution would save if it deters more than imprisonment. Asked whether they would execute murderers if each execution were to deter ten murders, thereby saving ten innocent lives, all abolitionists I have questioned answer in the negative.

The vulgar argument that holds execution to be wrong, because it does to the murderer what he did to his victim, neglects to note that many punishments do to the criminal what he did to his victim. In the past this was thought to be the essence of justice. The difference between a crime and a punishment is social, not physical. There is no need for physical dissimilarity. A crime is an unlawful act, legal punishment is a lawful act. Taking a person from his family and confining him against his will in a small cell may be an unlawful kidnaping, or a lawful arrest. The difference is not physical. Neither is the difference between murder and execution, or being fined and being robbed.

There is no evidence for brutalization caused by the death penalty. The idea that legal killing will lead to imitation by illegal killing, or to any increase in violent crime, is unsubstantiated. And proponents do not explain why legal imprisonment does not lead to kidnapings, or why violent crime in Singapore and Saudi Arabia, both renowned for executions and physical punishments, is so infrequent.

The idea that legal killing will lead to imitation by illegal killing, or to any increase in violent crime, is unsubstantiated.

The brutalization argument might be somewhat more valid against televising executions, although there are more salient arguments against televising. The executions would be sandwiched between sitcoms, sports, advertisements, contests and popular songs. The effect would be not so much to brutalize as to trivialize executions. Until two hundred years ago they served as popular entertainment. *Tempora mutantur et nos mutamur in illis*—we should not go back to using punishments as entertainment. Moreover, TV could show how the murderer is deprived of his life, but not what he did to his victim. The uninformed would be unduly stirred to pity for the criminal rather than the victim. . . .

We have more than 20,000 homicides annually, but only about 300 death sentences (and less than 50 executions). At this rate most of the about 3,000 murderers now on death row are far more likely to die of old age than by execution. On the average convicts spend more than eight years appealing their convictions. This seems a long time. Many appeals are repetitious as well as frivolous. Despite elaborate precautions, nothing short of abolishing punishment can avoid miscarriages altogether. The salient question about the death penalty is not: Could innocents be executed by mistake? (The answer is yes—courts are fallible) but: Does the death penalty save more innocent lives than it takes? Is there a net gain or loss?

Many desirable social practices cannot avoid killing innocents by accident. For instance, ambulances save many lives, but also run over some pedestrians. We do not abolish ambulances, because they save more innocents than they kill. So does the death penalty, if it deters some murders, as is likely, and if the miscarriages are few, as is likely too. It seems safer then, to rely on executions, which through deterrence, may save innocent lives, than it would be not to execute and risk not saving an indefinite number of innocents who could have been saved. If we execute a convicted murderer and his execution does not produce additional deterrence, his execution, though just, would not have been useful. But if his execution deters prospective murderers, not executing him would sacrifice innocent people who would have been spared had he been executed. . . .

The "root" of criminality

Perhaps college education helps explain opposition to the death penalty. Students are taught, accurately, that the great majority of criminals, including murderers, were mistreated and abused as children. Students infer, incorrectly, that mistreatment is the cause, or "root," of criminality. Unfortunately, they are not taught that the majority of mistreated and abused children do not become criminals, let alone murderers. Mistreatment and abuse are neither necessary nor sufficient causes of murder. To be sure, poverty, lack of education, childhood abuse, and, more important perhaps, the absence of a law-abiding family, may dispose to crime more than affluence and suburban living. But the former circumstances do not make it impossible to avoid crime. The responsibility for it remains with the individual who volunteers for crime.

The threat of punishment is meant precisely to deter persons who, for whatever reason, are disposed to crime. The legal threat is not needed for others. The so called causes of crime are, at best, explanations, but neither justifications nor excuses, let alone exculpations. Causes are exculpatory only if they compel crime and thus eliminate responsibility. It is reasonable to assume that there are some exceptional factors in the background of murderers, since murder is an exceptional action. Such factors may help explain criminal acts. They cannot exculpate.

Anatole France[2] sarcastically remarked "the law in its majestic equality prohibits rich and poor alike to steal bread or to sleep under bridges," implying that the rich are hardly tempted to commit the crimes that may

2. real name Jacques Anatole François Thibault, late nineteenth- and early twentieth-century French literary figure

be nearly, but not quite, irresistible to the poor. No one any longer arrests the homeless who sleep under bridges, nor a hungry person who steals bread. Still, the law is meant to prohibit stealing by those tempted by their circumstances as well as by those who are not. For the latter the prohibition is academic, for the former burdensome. Is this unjust, as Anatole France suggests? Hardly. Although its prohibitions apply to everyone, the criminal law necessarily burdens mainly those who by their circumstances are tempted to do what it prohibits. They are the ones that need to be deterred. There would be no need for criminal laws if no one were tempted to break them. And, surely, the most disadvantaged groups are most tempted to engage in unlawful acts, since they have the fewest legitimate resources to fulfill their desires. The prohibition of stealing imposes a greater burden on the poor than on the rich. But the greater temptation does not justify yielding to it.

Education tends to influence most those who get most of it, the professional classes. In modern times education may induce students to regard nothing as final and to feel that no decision ever should be. Since showing that the earth is not flat science has undermined many certainties and sewn many doubts. Thus the uneasiness about certainty among the educated. Death is and remains final. However, inflicting death as a final punishment which cuts off the future and any possibility of change seems psychologically in conflict with the spirit of the times imbued as it is by doubtfulness. Death is certain and we cannot abolish it. However, we can abolish the death penalty. The spirit which prevails among the educated elite pushes us to do so. The finality of the death penalty makes us uncomfortable. Never mind that the death penalty does not create death but merely hastens it. People like to ignore death—which the penalty makes hard to do. Moreover, extreme moral blame attaches to capital punishment—and we like even our courts and judges to be non-judgmental. It follows that, if present trends continue, the death penalty is likely to become more rare. Yet, history does not allow any trend to continue forever. Prediction is chancy. Still it seems likely currently that the death penalty will continue in America, Asia and Africa but is unlikely to be reinstituted in most of Europe where it has been abolished. . . .

Abolition of the death penalty would promise prospective murderers that we will never do to them what they will do to their victims.

Many criminologists believe deterrence requires that prospective criminals calculate the advantages of crime and compare them with the disadvantages, including punishment. Criminals usually do not do that. Nor does deterrence theory require that they calculate. To be sure, criminals volunteer for the risk of punishment because they expect a net advantage from crime. But they calculate no more than law abiding persons calculate to remain law abiding. Society offers disincentives to law breakers and incentives to law abiding persons. These incentives and disincentives powerfully contribute to the formation of law abiding or law breaking habits. But few people calculate. Law abiding people habitually ignore criminal opportunities. Law breakers habitually discount the risk of punishment. Neither calculates. Both follow habits largely produced by the incentives and disincentives society offers, which have different effects on different individuals in different circumstances. Once these habits are ingrained they are followed almost independently of new incentives and disincentives. The major impact of criminal justice is on habit formation, not on habits already formed. Most of our behavior arises from habits which are seldom explicitly calculated. One must be careful, then, not to confuse the rational reconstruction of one's behavior with the processes that actually lead to it.

Sundry arguments for abolition

Turn now to sundry arguments for abolition, some more popular than valid. The French writer Albert Camus insists that "a man is undone by waiting for capital punishment well before he dies. Two deaths are inflicted on him, the first being worse than the second, whereas he killed but once." (Would it follow that, had he murdered two persons, capital punishment would have been just?) The mistake Camus makes is in his belief, shared by many abolitionists, that the pain inflicted on the murderer should not exceed that of his victim. This limit derives from the limit the *lex talionis* set for retaliation or compensation. But the *lex talionis* regarded as torts acts we consider crimes. Camus' reasoning might govern tort rules for compensation. But criminal law must not be confused with tort law. Punishment for a crime is neither compensation nor retaliation, but retribution, as threatened by law, for the harm inflicted on the social order. Retribution need not be limited to, or be equal to the suffering of crime victims.

A somewhat frivolous argument alleges that life imprisonment without parole would cost less than execution. The argument is of doubtful relevance and accuracy. If one correctly calculates the cost of life imprisonment for murderers, who must be held in expensive high security prisons, it seems no less than the cost of execution. (Most murderers are young and likely to spend a long time in prison.) On the other hand, the cost of execution has been greatly inflated by the very persons who complain about it. They insist on lengthy procedures which add far more to cost than to justice. Frivolous appeals could be reduced with considerable savings. The cost of execution is currently estimated at about $2.5 million. If one assumes a cost of $30,000–40,000 for a year in high security prison and adds the cost of legal appeals (lifers keep their attorneys busy) and further assumes an average of forty years in prison, the cost is about the same whether we execute or incarcerate for life. But, as mentioned, the cost of execution is far higher than required by justice.

Some technical advantages of the death penalty should not be overlooked. By threatening it, prosecutors may persuade accomplices to testify against murderers, or persuade the murderers themselves to plead guilty in exchange for a life sentence. Also, in a hostage situation police can promise the criminal that the prosecution will not ask for the death penalty if he releases his hostages. Without the death penalty the criminal can threaten to kill his victims, while police can only threaten incarceration.

Religious objections to the death penalty reflect the Zeitgeist more than theology. In his *Summa Theologica* philosopher and theologist Thomas Aquinas writes: "a man shall be sentenced to death for crimes of irreparable harm." In his *Summa Contra Gentiles* Thomas points out that "[murderers] may be justly executed. . . . [T]hey also have, at the critical point of death, the opportunity to be converted to God through repentance." (They did not give this opportunity to their victims.)

Trendy abolitionists often conflate two different virtues, justice and charity. They must be distinguished. Justice tries to mete out what is deserved. Charity impels us to love and help regardless of desert. Religion enjoins compassion and forgiveness, even of murderers, but does not suggest that justice should be replaced by compassion. Scripture presents God as legislator and judge who imparts *Justitia Misericordiae Dulcore Temperata:* Justice tempered by mercy, but not replaced by it.

Abolition of the death penalty would promise prospective murderers that we will never do to them what they will do to their victims. Such a promise seems unwise as well as immoral.

4

Capital Punishment Encourages the Taking of Life

Mark Costanzo

Mark Costanzo is a professor of psychology at Claremont McKenna College in Claremont, California, and author of Just Revenge, *from which the following excerpt was taken.*

Capital punishment stimulates murder rather than deterring it. Strong evidence supports the theory of brutalization—that capital punishment lowers society's respect for life and leads to murder. Indeed, the homicide rate increases after executions, especially after well-publicized executions. The evidence suggests that state-sanctioned murder sends the message that it is acceptable to take the life of an individual who has done harm.

Deterrence theorists have always naively assumed that the threat of the death penalty would suppress the murder rate. The evidence indicates they are wrong. Of course, logic suggests three other possibilities: (1) the death penalty has no effect on murder rates; (2) the death penalty increases the number of murders; and (3) the death penalty deters some types of murder and stimulates other types. It is the second possibility, known as brutalization, that we now turn to.

From the beginning, public officials saw signs that the death penalty does not deter. During public executions in early America and Europe, pickpockets feverishly worked the crowds, even though picking pockets was a crime punishable by death. "The thieves selected the moment when the strangled man was swinging above them as the happiest opportunity, because they knew that everybody's eyes were on that person and all were looking up." The thieves somehow failed to absorb the intended message of the execution.

Not only did the bloody public executions of the past fail to deter, they churned up great violence in their wake. That was the principal reason why, despite great popularity, executions were removed from public

Excerpted from *Just Revenge*, by Mark Costanzo (New York: St. Martin's Press, 1997). Copyright © 1997 by Mark Costanzo. Reprinted by permission of the publisher.

view. Public executions were the scenes of drunkenness, revelry, fighting, and rioting. From the beginning, the spectacle of killing has brought out the worst in people and brought out the worst people. After standing among the spectators at a public execution in 1849, Charles Dickens described the scene:

> I believe that a sight so inconceivably awful as the wickedness and levity of the immense crowd collected at that execution this morning could be imagined by no man. . . . The horrors of the gibbet and of the crime which brought the wretched murderers to it faded in my mind before the atrocious bearing, looks, and language of the assembled spectators . . . thieves, low prostitutes, ruffians, and vagabonds of every kin, flocked on the ground with every variety of offensive and foul behavior.

The incendiary potential of executions

The wardens of modern American prisons have long recognized the incendiary potential of executions. Disciplinary problems and violent incidents rise during the days leading up to and following an execution. And the disruptive effects sometimes reach beyond the prison walls. Especially when an infamous killer is executed, rowdy crowds gather near the prison to cheer in approval when the death is announced. It is for these reasons that modern executions are held without fanfare, in the middle of the night when most people are asleep. Unseen executions create fewer disturbances. Public officials *say* they believe that executions deter, but they *act* as if they believe that executions brutalize.

Public officials say *they believe that executions deter, but they* act *as if they believe that executions brutalize.*

Like hypotheses about deterrence, hypotheses about brutalization can be tested. A careful examination of the data collected to evaluate deterrence theory should reveal whether brutalization occurs. If there is validity to the claim that executions brutalize, murder rates ought to rise after executions. In a series of articles and books on precisely this question, the respected death-penalty scholar William Bowers has examined data from nearly seventy different studies of murder rates. His conclusion is that executions do increase murder rates and that "this effect is slight in magnitude (though not in consequence), that it occurs within the first month or two of an execution, and that it dissipates thereafter." This small but consequential impact amounts to an average increase of one to four extra murders in the weeks after an execution. Bowers uncovered another intriguing trend: Although the number of murders tends to rise after any execution, the rise is greater when the execution is well publicized.

It appears that executions do communicate an important message. It just isn't the message lawmakers intend to communicate. Apparently the salient lesson is not "If you take a life you will lose your life" but instead, "It is acceptable to take the life of someone who has committed an egregious wrong against you." In fact, Bowers argues that the process of identification is likely to work in exactly the opposite direction from the one proposed by deterrence theory: "The potential murderer may equate someone who has greatly offended him—someone he hates, fears, or both—with the executed criminal. . . . Indeed, he himself may identify with the state as avenger; the execution may justify and reinforce his resolve to exact lethal vengeance."

Aggression and imitation

The psychology of brutalization is not yet entirely understood, but there are clues in the research on aggression and imitation. Perhaps people with a loose grip on sanity are the ones most influenced by an execution. Media accounts of the execution and stories about the condemned man may bring violent images and ideas to the minds of a few susceptible and potentially violent people. Some of these people may become morbidly obsessed with a murder. For those people who are already primed and ready to act violently, fascination with a murder or an execution may be enough to push barely repressed impulses to the surface. Some sociologists and psychiatrists have suggested that persons haunted by self-loathing may even see execution as a means of escape rather than as a dreaded punishment. For such people, the benefits of murder may become salient. "With the crime that leads to execution, the offender also strikes back at society or particular individuals. The execution will, of course, satisfy a guilt-inspired desire for punishment, and may also be seen as providing the opportunity to be seen and heard, an occasion to express resentment, alienation, and defiance." Clearly, many murderers enjoy their time in the spotlight.

Although the psychological process by which executions stimulate murders needs more exploration, the finding of brutalization is far more consistent with the evidence than is deterrence theory. Certainly, we know that other forms of violence beget more violence: The assassination of President John F. Kennedy boosted the homicide rate, and highly publicized suicides, like that of actor Marilyn Monroe, provoked a substantial increase in suicides. And, like the brutalization effect produced by executions, the effects of assassinations and suicides subside after a month or two. The impact of all forms of violence is magnified when the violence receives greater publicity.

> *All but the most irrational supporters of capital punishment have lost faith in deterrence.*

Even if there is a deterrent effect (perhaps for the tiny percentage of murders that are calm and calculated), it is overshadowed by the destructive effects of brutalization. If a few innocent lives are saved, many more innocent lives are sacrificed. And if executions lead to the taking of innocent lives, surely the practice of killing murderers should be judged immoral, especially for those whose support of the death penalty rests on the belief that it saves lives.

A sanitized reason

All but the most irrational supporters of capital punishment have lost faith in deterrence. Those who genuinely believe in deterrence theory will usually abandon their belief when they become aware of the impressive evidence refuting it. But there has always been another group whose professed faith in deterrence was disingenuous. For this group, deterrence is merely a socially acceptable, sanitized reason for supporting the death penalty. Deterrence theory allows them to cloak themselves in rationality and conceal the underlying reasons for their support. Research has now stripped away that cloak and exposed the real reasons for their support of the death penalty: rage and revenge.

On the eve of an execution in his state, the governor of California, Pete Wilson, expressed a sentiment often repeated by supporters of the death penalty: "The death penalty is worth having even if it only saves a single innocent life." Is the converse also true? Should the death penalty be abolished if it incites the taking of a single innocent life?

5

Capital Punishment Can Deter Juvenile Violence

Chris Lindorfer

Chris Lindorfer is a mother of five living in California.

To protect the public and affirm the value of human life, the death penalty should be reconsidered as the standard punishment for murder, even if it is perpetrated by a juvenile. The cold, premeditated homicides carried out by youths in recent years should not be condoned. Capital punishment is needed to make these violent youths pay for their crimes, prevent them from committing other offenses, and to deter other youths from committing murder. The juvenile justice system must implement the death penalty in order to end this disturbing trend of juvenile violence.

How can murder be taken seriously, if the penalty isn't equally as serious? A crime, after all, is only as severe as the punishment that follows it. As the former mayor of New York City Edward Koch once said: "It is by exacting the highest penalty for the taking of human life, that we affirm the highest value of human life." Our society needs to reconsider the death penalty as the standard punishment for murder. To deter crime and make the death penalty more effective we should not condone murders that children between 11–17 commit.

Executions of juveniles began in 1642 with Thomas Granger, Plymouth Colony, MA. In the more than 350 years since that time, approximately 346 persons have been executed for juvenile crimes. The current age of juvenile offenders on death row range between nineteen and thirty nine. Since the reinstatement of the death penalty in 1976, there have only been 9 executions of inmates sentenced for juvenile crimes.

Children who kill

Statistics obtained for the US Department of Justice, Bureau of Justice Statistics, maintains that 13 percent of the death row population were under the age of nineteen, at the time of arrest. They also state that 2.2 percent of the population were seventeen or under at the time of arrest. As of December 31, 1997, there were 67 juvenile arrests on death row. Their time there, ranges between two weeks to over 19 years. All 67 were there for murder and their total victim count was 89. These are more than just statistics, these are children who kill.

On September 2, 1996, Barry Loukaitis, a 14 year old honor student in Moses Lake, Washington, broke into an algebra class with a high powered rifle and shot three students and their teacher. Two of the students and their teacher died.

To deter crime and make the death penalty more effective we should not condone murders that children between 11–17 commit.

In 1996, 11 year old Ray Martin Deffered, was charged with eight counts of murder after setting a lethal fire in a suburban apartment complex, west of Portland, Oregon. The fire killed eight people, including a teenage mother and her newborn child.

On October 1, 1997, Luke Woodham, opened fire on a room full of schoolmates at Pearl High School, killing two and wounding seven. Luke, a sophomore, started his day, by slitting his mother's throat before heading to school in her car, with a rifle tucked under his trench coat. Witnesses stated he then walked to an atrium crowded with hundreds of students and started blasting at "anybody he could find."

On December 1, 1997, a high school freshman, Michael Carneal, went on a deadly rampage, killing three fellow students and wounding five others. Carneal, a self-professed atheist, shot 11 rounds into a Morning Prayer Circle in the lobby of his Paducah, Kentucky High School. The boy had in his possession three spare clips of ammunition and four guns.

In a new trend, that's turning rural schools into the post offices of the 90's, on March 24, 1998, Michael Johnson and Andrew Golden, heavily armed and dressed in camouflage, opened fire on classmates and teachers in Jonesboro, Arkansas, killing five and wounding 10. The two boys laid in hiding in the woods behind their school and started taking down students as they exited during a fake fire alarm. The boys were caught heading for a white van where they had more guns and ammunition. The van was also their planned escape.

When police searched the pockets of 11 year old Andrew's camouflage fatigues, they found 312 shells, two speed loaders, a rifle, and two hand guns. On 13 year old Michael, they found a 30.06, Remington rifle with a round in the chamber, four other guns and 142 rounds of ammunition. Items in the mini van included a camouflage jacket, a military duty belt with a 10 inch survival knife, four other knives, insulated vest, crossbow, plastic tool box filled with food items, a propane torch, assorted ammunition, and Michael's hunters education card.

The day prior to the shooting, both boys had warned classmates of the impending danger, making statements like "Tomorrow you will find out if you live or die." Yet, even before that, a counselor had talked to Michael about telling another young boy that he wanted to "shoot up the school." But Michael passed it off as a dream in which he died, and it scared him so he wouldn't do it. Yet the rebel and the choir boy did do it. These children entered the ranks of mass murderers.

One of the requirements for the death penalty, is that the crime be carried out with malice aforethought. These were children who knew what they were doing. They thought out, planned and executed it with more thought and preparation than many adults. They had a motive, acquired the means, and carried out the execution of five others. Their murders were in cold blood, premeditated, and wrong. Under Arkansas law, they are too young to be tried as adults. They can only be held as juvenile delinquents until the age of 18. According to one witness, "These two are cold blooded, evil children, and I don't care how bad that sounds. The four girls who died don't get to start over."

The death penalty makes perfect sense

I felt it necessary at this point to ask for input from a youth to see if the severity of what was done was understood, on a level equal with the children committing these crimes. I found that in cases, they did understand and felt that the punishment should fit the crime.

Juveniles will continue to commit crime as long as they feel it is in their best interest. The purpose of our current juvenile justice system is to protect the public and the public safety. It is supposed to promote the concept of punishment for criminal acts. To remove, where appropriate, the taint of criminality from children committing certain crimes, and to provide for treatment, training, and rehabilitation. To achieve this, the juvenile justice system needs to make the crime "Not in the child's best interest." In other words, the punishment for the crime must be harsh enough to deter the juvenile from committing the crime. Under this, the death penalty makes perfect sense. Here is a punishment that truly makes the violent juvenile pay for his crime, stops him from committing future crimes, and deters other juveniles from committing the same crime. When considering the death penalty, both its merits and its faults, we need to keep in sight, the victims.

6

Capital Punishment May Encourage Juvenile Violence

Philip Brasfield

Philip Brasfield is a contributing editor for The Other Side, *a bimonthly nondenominational Christian journal. He has been in prison for more than twenty years.*

In recent years, shocking episodes of violent juvenile crime and homicide have left the nation struggling to understand why seemingly normal youths would commit such terrible acts of violence. One explanation is that these teens have tragically followed the state's example. When the state executes its own citizens to address crime, it risks teaching children that murder can be justifiably used to solve society's problems.

> *"It is the deed that teaches, not the name we give it. Murder and capital punishment are not opposites that cancel one another but similars that breed their kind."*
>
> *—George Bernard Shaw*

The rash of violent crimes committed in 1998 by juveniles shocked the nation. Our alarm increases with each new report of the location, body count, and young ages of the children involved.

The entire nation was horrified in the spring of 1998 when two boys aged twelve and fourteen opened fire on their schoolmates in Jonesboro, Arkansas, killing a teacher and four students and wounding ten other students. Similar episodes have unfolded in 1998 in Mississippi, Oregon, and Kentucky. The tremors created by these crimes have shaken us all, including those of us locked away here in this Texas prison.

We are all left struggling to comprehend the rage that underlies such crimes. What would motivate seemingly normal children to perpetrate such violence?

Given the shock and anger surrounding these crimes, it's not surprising that in Texas (the death-penalty capital of the Western world) a legislator has proposed a new crime bill that would lower the age at which one can be executed to eleven years old. Representative Jim Pitts, himself the father of a fifth-grader, claims his office received hundreds of phone calls after he introduced the bill: "About 60 percent in favor and 40 percent against." Referring to the many supporters of the bill, Pitts comments, "These are not the 'Leave It to Beaver' types I grew up with." [The bill was not passed.]

I suppose a lot of folks in and out of prison have been battered beyond the healing honesty of tears. The voices on talk radio argue more about the age at which kids reach moral and legal responsibility for their actions than about why we continue to arm ourselves more than any other Western country. Have we convinced ourselves that we are immune to the inevitable backlash of violence against others throughout our history?

Many states continue to aggressively extend their use of the death penalty to cover more cases and younger ages, without any evidence that such measures will reduce the violence.

Charlie Rumbaugh was one of the first friends I made on death row, and the first "juvenile offender" I knew who was condemned to die. A reform-school runaway, he'd robbed and killed an aging jeweler in Amarillo. Because of his violent past in the juvenile system, Charlie was tried as an adult—and sentenced to death.

Charlie was the first one to tell you he was guilty—and that he knew exactly what *guilty* meant. For most of us, *guilty* is a word used to justify blame. But *guilty* is also a feeling of immense weight, a spiritual burden that grows heavier with time. Charlie carried that burden throughout his time in prison.

As almost always happens, the man that Charlie Rumbaugh became while waiting to be executed was a far cry from the scared, dumb runaway who shot and killed another human. In prison, confronting the realities of life and death, he became a better person than he'd ever thought possible. His execution several years ago ended his dream of working to help the kind of kid he'd once been.

The death penalty acquires a human face

Support for the death penalty has always been high here in Texas—around 70 percent. But in the aftermath of Karla Faye Tucker's execution in 1998, surveys revealed that the number of folks supporting the death penalty had dropped by more than 20 percent. Tucker's highly publicized case, and the days leading up to her execution, had given the death penalty a human face.

Tucker was a teenager when she participated in a pair of horrific and brutal murders. On death row, she confronted her own deep outrage and sorrow over her actions, and the shattering reality of how deeply human evil can reside in one's life. Christianity enabled her to make sense of her life and led her to become a different person.

Karla Faye Tucker lived her faith in prison, and it showed. She knew she could never change the fact that she had hacked two people to death with a pickaxe, but her faith assured her that she had been redeemed from the darkest depths and now lived "in the light."

Tucker's situation was hotly debated behind these walls, just as it was outside them. Many here believed Texas would never execute a woman. Others thought Texas governor George W. Bush might pardon her, because she was Christian—or maybe because he's one, too. Still others placed hope in the Board of Pardons and Paroles, even though it has never, since the reinstatement of the death penalty in 1972, commuted a death sentence based solely upon the petition of the condemned.

I argued all along that if ever Texas *had* to execute someone, it was Karla Faye. Failure to execute her because of her gender or religious faith would have opened the door to litigation from hundreds of male prisoners, including the many men on death row who claim a born-again faith in Christ. In the end, despite the outcry of religious leaders like Pat Robertson and Pope John Paul II, as well as thousands of plain folks, Karla Faye Tucker died for her sins.

Reducing crime, killing the death penalty

Of the 447 people on Texas's death row as I write this, twenty-seven were juveniles when convicted of murder. At the beginning of 1998, sixty-seven persons nationwide were awaiting execution for murders committed as juveniles. Many states continue to aggressively extend their use of the death penalty to cover more cases and younger ages, without any evidence that such measures will reduce the violence.

In light of the many studies that have noted *increases* in murder rates in the months following an execution, we have to wonder what kind of message our nation's willingness to kill its own citizens—even its children—is sending to our young people. As Michael Godfrey of the Center on Juvenile and Criminal Justice wrote in a recent study, "The state may be tragically leading by example."

Could this be so? Are the kids in Arkansas and Kentucky and Oregon and the rest of America watching what we allow the state to do in our names and following our tragic example? When the state takes a person out of a cage where it has held them for years and kills them "to solve a problem,"are the kids brutalized—even if the rest of society is too distracted or apathetic to notice?

If we are serious about reducing crime and violence in our country, then killing the death penalty is a place to begin. By ending, rather than expanding, the state-sanctioned violence of executions, we will teach our children to truly value all life.

7

Public Executions Can Maximize the Deterrent Effect of Capital Punishment

George J. Bryjak

George J. Bryjak is a professor of sociology at the University of San Diego.

Making the death penalty a public spectacle by televising executions would maximize the deterrent effect of capital punishment. Since deterrence relies on the theory that people will refrain from participating in homicide or crime if they perceive the threat of swift and certain punishment, the death penalty could be made a more effective deterrent if executions were televised and reached a large audience on a regular basis.

In 2001, U.S. Attorney General John Ashcroft announced that the June 11, 2001, execution of Timothy McVeigh would be televised via a live, encrypted, closed-circuit telecast and made available to the survivors of the Oklahoma City bombing as well as family members of the 168 victims. In light of this decision, we might ask ourselves why all state executions are not televised.

Although the number of Americans who advocate the death penalty has declined from 80 percent in 1994 to 67 percent in October 2000, the smaller figure still demonstrates strong support for capital punishment. Two of the reasons most often cited by death penalty proponents are (1) retribution—"an eye for an eye, a tooth for a tooth," and (2) general deterrence, that is, capital punishment will deter some would-be killers.

Maximize the death penalty's deterrent capacity

If as a nation we execute people in large measure because of our belief in the death penalty's deterrent capacity, then we should maximize that capacity by turning state-sanctioned deaths into public spectacles. Since 74 percent of all known homicide offenders between 1976 and 1999 were under 35 years of age (including 10.7 percent under 18) watching executions on television should be a mandatory component of the school curriculum beginning at an age when children can be tried and sentenced as adults (if not sooner). Minimally, just young males could be compelled to witness executions as females comprise only 10 percent of those arrested for murder.

If we honestly believe in the deterrent value of capital punishment, executions should be given the widest public audience.

Surely we cannot oppose children witnessing executions for fear of damaging their psycho-social development. By the time the typical American youth graduates from high school, he or she will have watched thousands of killings via television, many of them graphically and gruesomely portrayed.

If we honestly believe in the deterrent value of capital punishment, executions should be given the widest public audience. These state-sanctioned. events could be scheduled for prime-time television viewing; the first Tuesday of the month designated "execution day." Why not execute mass murderers, serial killers and other heinous offenders during a half-time extravaganza at the Super Bowl when half the nation is watching?

Although some studies have concluded that criminal homicides decline after well-publicized executions, most have found no effect, while still others have discovered that homicides actually increase after executions. This latter phenomenon is called the "brutalization effect" in that well-publicized executions desensitize people to the immorality of killing, thereby increasing the likelihood that some individuals will make the decision to kill.

In a major death penalty study published in 2000, Columbia University law professor James S. Liebman found that states with capital punishment (39) account for about 80 percent of the nation's homicide and 76 percent of the population. Although this is negative evidence for the deterrence perspective, arguably the number of homicides in these states would have been lower if the executions had been televised. The entire deterrence thesis rests on the premise that people will desist from criminal activity if they are made aware of the (high) certainty and severity of punishment for a given offense.

Advantages to public viewed executions

There are additional advantages to having public viewed executions. To begin, after a year or so of such fare, we might be asking ourselves some tough questions. For example, why are a disproportionate number of those individuals slated to die in some locales African-American?

A 1998 study found that black defendants in Philadelphia were almost four times more likely than other defendants convicted of committing identical crimes to receive the death penalty. In 1994, Supreme Court Justice Harry Blackmun stated that "Even under the most sophisticated death penalty statutes, race continues to play a major role in determining who shall live and who shall die."

Watching executions may give us pause to re-examine patterns of race-of-victim and race-of-defendant discrimination in sentencing. Of the 172 people executed between 1976 and 1998 for interracial murders, 11 were white offenders convicted of killing black victims, and 161 were black defendants convicted of killing white victims. More than 80 percent of capital cases involve white victims even though only 50 percent of murder victims are white. Why is the taking of a white life more deserving of the death penalty than the slaying of a non-white?

Civil rights leader Mohandas Gandhi opposed capital punishment stating that only God has the right to take a life, and, since human beings can never fully understand the motives and thinking of another person, we are not capable of making life-ending decisions. I am against capital punishment for these same reasons as well as the injustices rife in the implementation of this penalty.

However, I realize that because of strong public support the death penalty is likely to be part of the American criminal justice system for the indefinite future. So, we should follow Saudi Arabia's example and maximize the potential deterrent effect by making the executions public spectacles. If we are going to kill people for killing people, let us make the most of it.

8

Public Executions Will Not Deter Crime

Paul Finkelman

Paul Finkelman is the Chapman Distinguished Professor of Law at the University of Tulsa College of Law, Oklahoma.

In the past, executions were carried out in public in the hope of deterring crime. However, public executions were done away with because they degraded the morality of the public and often led to violent riots during which some onlookers were murdered. Moreover, public executions obviously did not deter crime, as evidenced by the plethora of petty thiefs who preyed on those watching the execution. In light of these facts, it cannot be expected that the most recent public execution, the closed-circuit telecast of the execution of Oklahoma City bomber Timothy McVeigh, will deter crime. On the contrary, many sick individuals will watch McVeigh's televised execution and see him as a martyr, perhaps inspiring them to follow in his steps.

The countdown has begun for the May 16, 2001, televised execution of America's most heinous criminal: Timothy J. McVeigh, the Oklahoma City bomber who killed 168 people, including 19 children. [He was executed by lethal injection on June 11, 2001.]

Televising McVeigh's death will become the latest wrinkle in reality TV and it will surely raise the stakes in the capital punishment game. How long will it be before we're able to watch executions in the privacy of our homes or at the local sports bar?

And will we ever be satisfied with another group of handpicked publicity seekers marooned on a desert island when we can watch criminals die?

In 1936, onlookers drank sodas and ate hot dogs when this nation's last public execution was held in Owensboro, Kentucky.

Recently, Attorney General John Ashcroft approved a closed-circuit telecast of McVeigh's execution for bombing the Alfred P. Murrah Federal Building on April 19, 1995.

Ashcroft's decision fulfills the requests of about 285 victims and family members who want to see McVeigh die. It also brings us closer to the time when it was good, clean fun to watch people beheaded, hanged or burned at the stake.

More than 1,100 victims' relatives and survivors were asked whether they wanted to see McVeigh die by lethal injection. About 800 said they did not want to see him strapped to a gurney and injected with poison. Some said they want him to die, but don't feel compelled to watch it, and others said they want him to spend the rest of his life behind bars.

Ashcroft says federal authorities will take steps to prevent recording or pirating of the telecast. But it is reasonable to presume that the execution will turn out to be more public than Ashcroft intends.

The public execution was supposed to make the community feel better while simultaneously acting as a deterrent to crime. But neither happened.

Security experts say it will be difficult, but not impossible, to intercept and decode the telecast so it can be taped and sold on cassettes or shown on the web. It might even wind up on network television. Imagine the ratings for McVeigh's execution during sweeps week.

Meanwhile, the lawsuits have begun. In April 2001, a federal judge rejected an Internet company's request to show live video of McVeigh's execution over the web.

The law barring cameras from executions was challenged by Entertainment Network Inc.(ENI), a Tampa, Florida, company that made its name with VoyeurDorm.com, which allowed viewers to watch the daily activities of female college students via 55 web cameras. ENI wanted to charge viewers $1.95 to watch McVeigh die in the execution chamber of the U.S. Penitentiary in Terre Haute, Indiana.

"The Constitution does not require that those who wish to record courts or executions be allowed to do so," an assistant U.S. attorney told a federal judge in Indianapolis. "The legislatures of every state that has executions, and the federal government, have decided that executions should not be public spectacles."

Expanded access

U.S. District Court Judge John Tinder ruled that the First Amendment does not entitle ENI to broadcast the execution on the Internet.

ENI chief executive David Marshlack said an appeal was planned. "The law is on our side and applying constitutional precedent to this case, we should have won," an ENI attorney said.

More lawsuits are likely to follow. Reporters will surely seek access to watch and record the reactions of those who see the closed-circuit broadcast at a Bureau of Prisons facility in Oklahoma City.

Why shouldn't the execution be broadcast nationally? All Americans were deeply harmed by McVeigh as we watched in horror while the dead were pulled from the rubble. Let us all see his final minutes.

Televise the execution for public consumption, and let the entire world see how the United States deals with its worst criminals.

The Saudi Arabians will understand. They still behead people in public. The North Koreans, Chinese, Iraqis, and residents of various other benighted dictatorships will smile, happily noting that the United States has descended to their level of brutality.

But many in the civilized world will be shocked. They will shake their heads in wonder that a nation so rich, so powerful, so seemingly modern, can be living in another age.

The execution frenzy is already building in Terre Haute, the western Indiana town where the nation's only federal death chamber is located.

Terre Haute's mayor, Judith A. Anderson, recently told the *New York Times* that she is already fielding requests from hawkers who want to sell T-shirts and buttons. "We have no control over what they sell. We're just asking that it be in very good taste," she said.

Meanwhile, thousands of outsiders—members of the news media, protesters, curiosity seekers and peddlers—are expected to descend on the town as the execution date approaches.

Although McVeigh will die behind prison walls, the execution is creating a carnival atmosphere similar to that of public executions of bygone days. Televising it on closed circuit only contributes to the surreal atmosphere.

Entertainment, not deterrence

Up through much of the 19th century, public executions were common in the United States, Great Britain and many other countries.

The purpose of the public execution was to impress upon the masses the evil of certain crimes, and to demonstrate the ultimate penalty for committing them. The public hanging, or beheading, or burning at the stake, was meant to strike fear in the heart of the would-be criminal.

The next sick, angry, pathetic bomber, will see [Timothy] McVeigh as a martyr.

Usually the execution was preceded by a sermon and a prayer, and often with the public confession of the condemned. With rope around his or her neck, the condemned would ask forgiveness of the people and of God for the crime. God's justice and man's justice were tied together.

The public execution was supposed to make the community feel better while simultaneously acting as a deterrent to crime. But neither happened, and in 1868 Great Britain halted public executions. During the 19th century, they began to be hidden from the public's eye in the United States.

Logically, if Ashcroft believes McVeigh's execution should be broadcast, he should allow us all to see it.

After all, the rationale for public executions was that they deterred crime. The minister's sermon, the condemned man's confession and repentance, the body swinging from the scaffold, legs kicking, were part of the civics lesson.

That was the theory. In reality, most public executions were ghoulish, carnival-like spectacles that sometimes turned into violent riots. On more than one occasion, these riots led to the death of onlookers.

Nor did they deter crime. In 18th-century England, while small-time purse snatchers were being hanged, other criminals often were busy picking the pockets and cutting the purses of those watching the execution. So much for the moral lesson of public execution.

It seemed that we had learned a lesson: Public executions served no purpose except to entertain the masses, and they lowered public morality and good taste. Now we are ready to charge back to darker times, but with a high-tech, modern twist—closed-circuit television.

Will McVeigh's execution act as a deterrent?

History and logic suggest not. More likely, the next Timothy McVeigh, the next sick, angry, pathetic bomber, will see McVeigh as a martyr. Even a televised execution with a limited audience is a victory for McVeigh and those who are waiting to imitate him. And in the end, his death will only bring out the worst in us.

9

Capital Punishment Protects Public Safety More Effectively than Does Life Imprisonment

Wesley Lowe

Wesley Lowe is a test technician at Xerox and an advocate of capital punishment.

Capital punishment protects public safety much more effectively than does life in prison without parole. Convicts serving life sentences can still kill guards and other inmates. Moreover, convicts who escape often commit murder and other violent acts against innocent people. Additionally, when a murderer is sentenced to life without parole, it does not mean that he will carry out that entire sentence—the average prison sentence served for homicide is five years and eleven months. Laws and parole boards change over the years and convicted murders serving life may suddenly be eligible for parole. While a murderer is alive, there is always the chance that he or she will murder or harm an innocent person again.

Abolitionists claim that there are alternatives to the death penalty. They say that life in prison without parole serves just as well. Certainly, if you ignore all the murders criminals commit within prison when they kill prison guards and other inmates, and also when they kill decent citizens upon escape, like Dawud Mu'Min who was serving a 48-year sentence for the 1973 murder of a cab driver when he escaped a road work gang and stabbed to death a storekeeper named Gadys Nopwasky in a 1988 robbery that netted $4.00. Fortunately, there is now no chance of Mu'Min commiting murder again. He was executed by the state of Virginia on November 14, 1997.

Another flaw is that life imprisonment tends to deteriorate with the passing of time. Take the Moore case in New York State for example.

In 1962, James Moore raped and strangled 14-year-old Pamela Moss. Her parents decided to spare Moore the death penalty on the condition that he be sentenced to life in prison without parole. Later on, thanks to a change in sentencing laws in 1982, James Moore is eligible for parole every two years!

If Pamela's parents knew that they couldn't trust the state, Moore could have been executed long ago and they could have put the whole horrible incident behind them forever. Instead they have a nightmare to deal with biannually. I'll bet not a day goes by that they don't kick themselves for being foolish enough to trust the liberal sham that is life imprisonment and rehabilitation. (According to the US Department of Justice, the average prison sentence served for murder is five years and eleven months.)

Just not good enough

Putting a murderer away for life just isn't good enough. Laws change, so do parole boards, and people forget the past. Those are things that cause life imprisonment to weather away. As long as the murderer lives, there is always a chance, no matter how small, that he will strike again. And there are people who run the criminal justice system who are naive enough to allow him to repeat his crime.

Kenneth McDuff, for instance, was convicted of the 1966 shooting deaths of two boys and the vicious rape-strangulation of their 16-year-old female companion. A Fort Worth jury ruled that McDuff should die in the electric chair, a sentence commuted to life in prison in 1972 after the U.S. Supreme Court struck down the death penalty as then imposed. In 1989, with Texas prisons overflowing and state officials under fire from the federal judiciary, McDuff was quietly turned loose on an unsuspecting citizenry.

Within days, a naked body of a woman turned up. Prostitute Sarafia Parker, 31, had been beaten, strangled and dumped in a field near Temple. McDuff's freedom in 1989 was interrupted briefly. Jailed after a minor racial incident, he slithered through the system and was out again in 1990.

Life imprisonment tends to deteriorate with the passing of time.

In early 1991, McDuff enrolled at Texas State Technical College in Waco. Soon, Central Texas prostitutes began disappearing. One, Valencia Joshua, 22, was last seen alive February 24, 1991. Her naked, decomposed body later was discovered in a shallow grave in woods behind the college. Another of the missing women, Regenia Moore, was last seen kicking and screaming in the cab of McDuff's pickup truck. During the Christmas holidays of 1991, Colleen Reed disappeared from an Austin car wash. Witnesses reported hearing a woman scream that night and seeing two men speeding away in a yellow or tan Thunderbird. Little more than two months later, on March 1, 1992, Melissa Northrup, pregnant with a third child, vanished from the Waco convenience store where she worked. McDuff's beige Thunderbird, broken down, was discovered a block from the store.

Fifty-seven days later, a fisherman found the young woman's nearly nude body floating in a gravel pit in Dallas County, 90 miles north of Waco. By then, McDuff was the target of a nationwide manhunt. Just days after Mrs. Northrup's funeral, McDuff was recognized on television's "America's Most Wanted" and arrested May 4 in Kansas City.

For people who truly value public safety, there is no substitute for the best in its defense which is capital punishment.

In 1993, a Houston jury ordered him executed for the kidnap-slaying of 22-year-old Melissa Northrup, a Waco mother of two. In 1994, a Seguin jury assessed him the death penalty for the abduction-rape-murder of 28-year-old Colleen Reed, an Austin accountant. Larry Pamplin, the sheriff of Falls County, appeared at McDuff's Houston trial for the 1992 abduction and murder of Melissa Northrup. "Kenneth McDuff is absolutely the most vicious and savage individual I know," he told reporters. "He has absolutely no conscience, and I think he enjoys killing." If McDuff had been executed as scheduled, he said, "no telling how many lives would have been saved."

At least nine, probably more, Texas authorities suspect.

His reign of terror finally ended on November 17, 1998, when Kenneth McDuff was put to death by the state of Texas by Lethal Injection. May his victims rest in peace.

No substitute

There has also been major political hay made out of a nasty scandal involving a prisoner named Willie Horton and Massachusetts' controversial "Prison Furlough Program." Former Massachussetts governor Mike Dukakis was genuinely committed to the program, and had worked hard to bolster it, despite serious public concerns. In 1976, he'd actually vetoed legislation that would have banned furloughs for first-degree murderers, defending the practice as an essential "management tool."

Thus, a decade later, in June of 1986, there was nothing in the law to deny convicted murderer Horton what was supposed to be a routine 48-hour leave.

Predictably, Horton didn't play by the rules. He fled, eventually arriving in Maryland, where, in April of 1987, he had pistol-whipped and knifed Clifford Barnes, then bound and gagged him and twice raped his fiancee, Angela. When the story of the furlough became known, Horton's brutality created a public uproar.

The Maryland judge who subsequently sentenced Horton to two consecutive life terms refused to extradite him to Massachusetts. "I'm not prepared to take the chance that Mr. Horton might again be furloughed ... This man should never draw a breath of free air again," said the judge.

The scandal heated to a rolling boil. In April of 1988, embattled Massachusetts legislators finally killed the 16-year-old program—without further resistance from Dukakis. Thank God!

This is why for people who truly value public safety, there is no substitute for the best in its defense which is capital punishment. It not only forever bars the murderer from killing again, it also prevents parole boards and criminal rights activists from giving him the chance to repeat his crime.

10

Capital Punishment Is an Ineffective Crime Control Policy

Gary W. Potter

Gary W. Potter is a professor in the Department of Justice and Police Studies at Eastern Kentucky University.

Overwhelming scientific evidence proves that the administration of capital punishment is counterproductive in the fight against crime. First, pursuing death penalty prosecutions and executing prisoners are much more costly than incarcerating prisoners for life. As a result, capital punishment diverts funds that could be spent on law enforcement, criminal justice agencies, and prisons. Second, capital punishment is not needed to keep murderers from killing again. When released from prison, the vast majority of prisoners convicted of violent crime do not murder again or even commit another serious crime. Last, capital punishment does not deter murder. Instead, it stimulates homicides and violence by desensitizing the public to the immorality of murder.

There is probably no public policy issue related to crime control that has been researched and studied over as long a period of time as the death penalty; in more varied ways than the death penalty; or in greater volume than the death penalty. Put simply, the dilemma is this: there is no crime control issue we know more about than the death penalty and there is no crime control issue where the scientific research has been more ignored by decision-makers and the public than the death penalty. The fact is that the death penalty debate is much more than a matter of conflicting opinions, morals, ethics, and values. There are a plethora of well established, scientifically documented facts at the disposal of both the public and lawmakers. These facts have emanated from research that has been replicated over and over again and subjected to the most rigorous scientific review process available. These facts are well beyond refutation. In sum, it is fair to say to a level of certainty that far exceeds the most rig-

Excerpted from Gary W. Potter's statement before the Joint Interim Health and Welfare Committee, Kentucky Legislature, March 20, 1999.

orous standards of proof in any court in America, that the death penalty, as presently constructed and administered is deplorably bad public policy. In studies using entirely different methodologies, at different times, in different places, constructing research questions in different ways, the facts are immutable and unchanging. The scientifically proven facts of the death penalty are clear. Those facts are:

1. The death penalty has no deterrent value to society. No evidence supporting either a general deterrent or a specific deterrent impact exists and no evidence supporting an incapacitation impact exists. The death penalty performs no crime control function whatsoever.
2. The death penalty, in fact, not only does not deter homicide and other crimes, but through a brutalization effect actually increases both homicide and violent crime markedly, seriously increasing the danger to society in states where it is used with any degree of frequency whatsoever.
3. The death penalty, even as constructed in post-*Furman*[1] statutes, is arbitrary, discriminatory and capricious in its application. The death penalty, in every jurisdiction, discriminates on the basis of race of offender, race of victim, gender, age, and socio-economic status.
4. The death penalty, as currently structured and administered, results in jury confusion and misinterpretation of the law at every stage of the process. This confusion seriously prejudices the defendant and results in both reversals on appeal and in a large number of wrongful convictions.
5. The death penalty, as currently structured and administered, results in the wrongful conviction and execution of the innocent at a level totally unacceptable in any civilized society.
6. The death penalty is enormously costly, strains the budgets of both state and local governments and diverts funds from more effective crime control strategies and victim assistance programs. This is true in all jurisdictions regardless of state statute. The cost of executions exceeds the cost of life imprisonment by a factor of better than two to one in every jurisdiction studied. And this enormous cost is borne by the taxpayers for a crime control policy that only makes violent crime worse. . . .

The cost of the death penalty

One of the least obvious, but most important problems with the death penalty is its enormous cost. Research on cost has consistently shown that pursuing a capital case is at least twice as costly as housing a convicted murderer for life in a high security correctional institution. Cost studies in North Carolina, Kansas, Texas, Kentucky, Nebraska and New York all show varying costs but similar ratios with regard to expense of death as a sentencing option:

1. In New York each death penalty trial costs $1.4 million compared with $602,000 for life imprisonment. The cost of imposing the

1. In the 1972 case of *Furman v. Georgia*, the Supreme Court eliminated federal and state capital punishment laws allowing wide discretion in the implementation of the death penalty.

death penalty in New York State has been estimated to be $3 million for each case.
2. In Florida the cost of each execution was estimated to be $3.2 million, about 6 times the amount needed to incarcerate a convicted murderer for life. From 1973 to 1988 Florida spent $57 million on the death penalty.
3. In Kentucky the cost of a capital trial varied between $2 and $5 million.
4. The most comprehensive study of the costs of the death penalty found that the state of North Carolina spends $2.16 million more per execution than for a non-capital murder trial resulting in imprisonment for life.
5. In California the death penalty adds $90 million annually to the costs of the criminal justice system. $78 million of that cost is incurred at the trial level.
6. The Judiciary Committee of the Nebraska legislature reported that any savings from executions are outweighed by the legal costs of a death penalty case. The report concluded that the death penalty does not serve the best interests of Nebraskans.
7. In Texas the cost of capital punishment is estimated to be $2.3 million per death sentence, three times the cost of imprisoning someone at the highest possible security level, in a single prisoner cell for 40 years.

Diverting money from other crime control

These high costs strain local and state budgets, divert money from other crime control and victim assistance programs, result in tax increases, prolong and extend the anguish of victims' families over years of appeals and successive execution dates, reduce other governmental services and often result in deferring salary increases for governmental employees:
1. In Indiana three recent capital cases cost taxpayers over $2 million just for defense costs. Prosecution costs usually exceed those of the defense.
2. In Washington State, officials were concerned in 1999 that costs for a single capital case would approach $1 million. The county in which the trial was held had to let one governmental position go unfilled, postponed employee pay hikes, drained the county's $300,000 contingency fund and eliminated all capital improvement projects for the fiscal year.
3. Thurston County in Washington budgeted $346,000 for 1999 alone, to seek Mitchell Rupe's third death sentence. Rupe is dying from liver disease and the state of Washington has had to undertake extreme measures to save Rupe from a natural death so that he may be executed. Since 1997, Thurston County has spent $700,000 just for the most recent sentencing hearing. [As of April 2002, Rupe was still alive.]
4. The state of Ohio spent over $1.5 million to execute one mentally ill man who was a death penalty volunteer. Some of the costs included $18,147 in overtime for prison employees and $2,250 in overtime for State Highway Patrol officers to provide support for

the execution. In addition the state had to pay overtime for 25 prison public information officers who worked the night of the execution. The state also spent $5,320 on a satellite truck so the official announcement of the execution could be beamed to outside media. Ohio's Attorney General had between 5 and 15 prosecutors working on the case, expending 10% of the state's annual budget for its capital crimes section, over a five year period. Keeping the man who was executed in prison for his entire life would have cost less than half as much.

5. Because of death penalty trial costs, Okanogan County, Washington had to delay pay raises for the county's 350 employees; could not replace two of four public health nurses in the county, and had to stop all non-emergency travel and put a hold on updating county computers and vehicles.

Negatively impacting criminal justice agencies

The death penalty also has a negative impact on the ability of criminal justice agencies to carry out their missions and perform their duties. The immense cost of the death penalty endangers the public in tangible and compelling ways as these examples indicate:

1. New Jersey laid off more than 500 police officers in 1991, at a time when it was putting into place a death penalty statute that would cost $16 million a year, more than enough to rehire all 500 officers.

2. In Florida, budget cuts resulting in a reduction of $45 million in funding for the Department of Corrections required the early release of 3,000 inmates while spending an estimated $57.2 million on executions.

3. Professors Richard Moran and Joseph Ellis estimated that the money it would take to implement the death penalty in New York for just five years would be enough to fund 250 additional police officers *and* build prisons for 6,000 inmates.

4. Ten other states also reported early release of prisoners because of overcrowding and underfunding. In Texas, the early release of prisoners has meant that inmates are serving only 20 percent of their sentences and re-arrests are common. On the other hand, Texas spent an estimated $183.2 million in just six years on the death penalty.

5. Georgia's Department of Corrections lost over 900 positions in 1998 and 1999 while local counties have had to raise taxes to pay for death penalty trials.

There are a large number of factors which come together to create the exceptionally high costs associated with the death penalty. First of all, both procedural and substantive constitutional safeguards put in place by the Supreme Court in death penalty cases drive up trial costs and the cost of appeals. As a result there is limited plea bargaining in death penalty cases (a factor which keeps down costs in all other prosecutions); there are lengthy pretrial motions; extensive investigations; increased use of expert witnesses; extensive voir dire; preemptory challenges; and extensive trial and appeal processes. Virtually none of these requirements are subject to reform or state recourse because they were necessitated by Supreme Court guidelines for the death penalty. In addition, almost every capital defendant in America is poor and taxpayers must invariably pay defense costs.

Let me emphasize two issues here:

1. While it is true that some of the costs of death penalty cases result from the appeal process the vast majority of the increased costs are front-end costs. That is, prosecutors spend much more on death penalty cases than on noncapital homicide cases. They reassign prosecutors from other cases, they divert monies for expert witnesses, jury consultants, additional investigation and legal research. This means that not only are enormous sums of money dedicated to death penalty prosecutions, but those moneys are diverted from literally dozens of other criminal cases.

2. The net effect of this front-end cost in capital prosecutions is that victims in many cases seen as less important by prosecutors' offices are not given adequate support or vigorous advocacy by the state. It also means that victim assistance programs, which should provide financial aid to victims, counseling for victims, and vital assistance in reconstituting their own lives are nonexistent and underfunded, all for the sake of a crime control policy which has no measurable social benefit.

In view of the fact, as we shall see in the next portion of my viewpoint, that scientific research can establish no incapacitative or deterrent benefit from the death penalty, this cost is entirely wasted.

General deterrence

The most commonly advanced argument in support of capital punishment has been that no offender wants to die, therefore the threat of execution will deter homicide in society at large. While this may seem a common sense fact, it is anything but sensible. The scientific facts are very simple. No credible study of capital punishment in the United States has ever found a deterrent effect.

In studies of contiguous states, at least one with the death penalty and at least one without, research has shown that there is no deterrent impact from capital punishment.

In studies of states where the death penalty was adopted or reinstated after having been abolished, research has once again failed to show any deterrent effect.

The death penalty performs no crime control function whatsoever.

Comparative data also fails to demonstrate any deterrent value to the death penalty. The United States is the only Western democracy that retains the death penalty. The United States also has, far and away, the highest homicide rate in the industrialized world.

Comparative data compiled by region within the United States shows the same pattern. According to data from the Bureau of Justice Statistics,

Southern states have consistently had the highest homicide rates in the country. In 1997, the South was the only region with a homicide rate above the national average, despite the fact that it accounts for 80% of all executions. The Northeast, which accounts for less than 1% of all executions in the U.S., has the lowest homicide rate. Similarly, when states with the death penalty are compared to those without the death penalty, the data show that a majority of death penalty states have homicide rates higher than non-death penalty states. In 1997 the average homicide rate for death penalty states was 6.6, while the average homicide rate for non-death penalty states was only 3.5.

The alleged deterrent value of the death penalty is refuted by all the data we have on violent crime. The death penalty, if it is to deter, must be a conscious part of a cost-benefit equation in the perpetrator's mind. There are very few murders that involve that level of rationality or consciousness of the outcomes. Most murders are (1) committed under the influence of drugs or alcohol; (2) committed by people with severe personality disorders; (3) committed during periods of extreme rage and anger; or (4) committed as a result of intense fear. None of these states of mind lend itself to the calm reflection required for a deterrent effect.

Specific deterrence

Some proponents of the death penalty argue that capital punishment provides a specific deterrent which controls individuals who have already been identified as dangerous criminal actors. According to this argument, the presence of the death penalty ought to reduce a wide variety of criminal acts. The weight of scientific evidence tells us that it does not.

The immense cost of the death penalty endangers the public in tangible and compelling ways.

If the death penalty deters homicide then it should prevent incarcerated people from killing again and reduce the number of homicides among prisoners. The fact of the matter is that over 90% of all prisoner homicides, killings of other prisoners or correctional officers, occur in states with capital punishment.

An extensive death penalty study, using multiple means of measurement that measured the impact of capital punishment in three distinct and different ways could find no evidence that the death penalty had any effect on felony crime rates, "this pattern holds for the traditional targeted offense of murder, the personal crimes of negligent manslaughter, rape, assault and robbery, as well as the property crimes of burglary, grand larceny, and vehicle theft. In other words, there is no evidence . . . that residents of death penalty jurisdictions are afforded an added measure of protection against serious crimes by executions," [states author W. Bailey].

Finally, it has been argued that capital punishment specifically protects law enforcement officers by deterring assaults on and killings of police. There have been five major studies addressing the question of whether capital punishment protects police officers. In no case did the death penalty provide any deterrent to killing law enforcement officers, nor did it reduce the rate of assaults on police.

Once again the scientific evidence is clear, the death penalty does not provide specific deterrence from other crimes. It has no deterrent impact on other felonies, it has no deterrent impact on crimes against law enforcement officers, it has no deterrent impact on drug crimes, and it has no deterrent impact on violent crimes. In fact, the death penalty is more likely to endanger the lives of police who investigate crime and pursue fugitives, and endanger the lives of witnesses who may provide evidence necessary for conviction. The reason is obvious, preventing capture and conviction becomes far more pressing a matter in death penalty states.

Incapacitation

Another frequently advanced argument is that the death penalty protects society by incapacitating violent criminals and thereby preventing further offenses. The evidence for this proposition is also weak. Obviously, an executed murderer is unlikely to recidivate, but so is a murderer in prison for life without parole. The facts, however, indicate that even if not executed and even if not incarcerated for life, it is unlikely that a person convicted of homicide will kill again, or even commit an additional serious offense.

A massive study which tracked the post-release behavior of 6,835 male prisoners serving sentences for homicide offenses, who were paroled from state institutions, found that only 4.5 percent of them were subsequently convicted of another violent crime and only 0.31 percent committed another homicide. This means that for every 323 executions we might prevent one additional murder. Other studies find essentially the same results. For example, a study of prisoners whose sentences were commuted as a result of the *Furman* decision found that 75 percent of these inmates committed no serious infractions of prison rules, and none of these inmates were involved in a prison homicide. Some of the *Furman*-commuted inmates were paroled back into the community. Only 14 percent of them committed a new crime, and only one committed an additional homicide.

[Authors] G. Vito, P. Koester and D. Wilson (1991) also analyzed the behavior of inmates removed from death row as a result of the *Furman* decision. Their study found that of those inmates eventually paroled only 4.5 percent committed another violent crime and only 1.6 percent committed another homicide. The authors conclude "that societal protection from convicted capital murderers is not greatly enhanced by the death penalty."

An extensive death penalty study . . . could find no evidence that the death penalty had any effect on felony crime rates.

Even in states with capital punishment the overwhelming majority of people convicted of homicide receive a prison sentence, and many of them will eventually be released on parole. A review of the data on these released murderers clearly reveal that they have the lowest recidivism rates of any felons. In addition, paroled murderers in states without the death penalty had a much lower rate of recidivism than parolees released in states with the death penalty.

The death penalty does not protect society from further crimes of violence in any way. Eleven additional studies from the National Criminal Justice Reference Service database for the period 1980–1998 all fail to find any general or specific deterrent or any incapacitive impact from the use of the death penalty.

The brutalization effect of the death penalty

Neither incapacitation nor deterrence theories are supported by the scientific research on capital punishment. In most public policy debates the burden of proof is on those advocating a measure to demonstrate its effectiveness. If that were the case in the death penalty debate adherents would fail miserably. But the fact is that the death penalty not only doesn't deter murder, it encourages people to kill.

Even if not executed and even if not incarcerated for life, it is unlikely that a person convicted of homicide will kill again, or even commit an additional serious offense.

Studies of capital punishment have consistently shown that homicide actually increases in the time period surrounding an execution. Social scientists refer to this as the "brutalization effect." Execution stimulates homicides in three ways: (1) executions desensitize the public to the immorality of killing, increasing the probability that some people will be motivated to kill; (2) the state legitimizes the notion that vengeance for past misdeeds is acceptable; and (3) executions also have an imitation effect, where people actually follow the example set by the state, after all, people feel if the government can kill its enemies, so can they.

Let me be clear here. The scientific evidence on the brutalization effect is compelling. We are not talking about one or two speculative studies. We are talking about a body of research that has found over and over again, in state after state, that the use of the death penalty increases, and often sharply increases, the number of homicides. Let me be specific:

1. *Oklahoma*: Oklahoma's return to capital punishment in 1990 was followed by a significant increase in killings that involved strangers, with an increase of one stranger homicide per month for the year following an execution. In addition, the analysis also showed a brutalization effect for total homicides as well as a variety of different types of killings that involved both strangers and nonstrangers.

2. *Arizona*: Studies in Arizona found an increase in specific types of homicides following an execution in that state. In particular the Arizona study found large increases in spur-of-the-moment homicides that involve strangers and/or arguments and a large increase in gun-related homicides.

3. *Georgia*: A study in Georgia found that a publicized execution is associated with an increase of 26 homicides, or 6.8 percent increase, in the month of the execution. Overall, publicized executions were associated with an increase of 55 homicides during the time period analyzed.
4. *Illinois*: A study of capital punishment in Illinois found that the net effect of executions was to increase rather than decrease Chicago first degree murders and total criminal homicides.
5. *California*: In California studies have found that the number of murders actually increased in the days prior to an execution and on the day of the execution itself. In addition homicide rates were even higher in the weeks after executions.
6. *Pennsylvania*: A study looking at data for both California and Pennsylvania found that each execution studied was followed by a two- to threefold increase in the number of homicides the next month. And in the earliest study demonstrating a brutalization effect, Robert Dann found an average increase of 4.4 homicides for each execution.

Once again the scientific research provides compelling evidence against the death penalty as public policy. The death penalty does, invariably and without exception increase the number of homicides in jurisdictions where it is applied. This has been proven in Pennsylvania, California, Oklahoma, Arizona, Illinois and other jurisdictions. The brutalization thesis is not mere speculation. It has been verified in study after study. If a legislature were looking at the impact of a pharmaceutical drug and only one study suggested that the drug killed more than it cured, legislators would no doubt ban the drug. The evidence with regard to the brutalization theory is far stronger, with at least eleven unrefuted, replicated and valid studies clearly showing a brutalization impact. In the case of the death penalty the cure is clearly worse than the disease, and like a dangerous drug, this cure should be banned.

The worst kind of crime-control policy

Criminologists and criminal justice scholars are constrained to make their judgments on facts and scientifically valid and reliable scholarly research. It is the judgment of the overwhelming majority of criminologists and criminal justice scholars that the death penalty is bad policy and is in fact criminogenic in its social impact. The American Society of Criminology (ASC), an organization made up of the best researchers and scholars in the country, has strongly condemned the death penalty:

> Be it resolved that because social science research has demonstrated the death penalty to be racist in application and social science research has found no consistent evidence of crime deterrence through execution, the ASC publicly condemns this form of punishment and urges its members to use their professional skills in legislatures and the courts to seek a speedy abolition of this form of punishment.

The scientific evidence on the death penalty is clear and unequivocal. The use of the death penalty in American society is the rough equivalent of a person hitting himself or herself repeatedly on the head with a hammer in order to treat a headache resulting from a brain tumor. It can only make a very bad situation much worse. This judgment is not based upon vague conceptions of morality or popular formulations of common sense or the vagaries of political opinion, it is based on rigorous evaluation of the state's two primary responsibilities: (1) to protect the public health and safety; and (2) to provide equity, fairness and justice to its citizens. The death penalty is anathema to both goals. It is the worst kind of crime-control policy.

11

Arguments for the Use of Capital Punishment as a Deterrent Are Flawed

Ernest Partridge

Ernest Partridge is a research associate in the Philosophy Department at the University of California, Riverside, and publishes the website "The Online Gadfly."

Supporters of capital punishment assert that capital punishment deters murder on the assumption that people's behavior can be influenced. Simultaneously, advocates also contend that convicted murderers deserve the death penalty on the assumption that human nature cannot be changed and thus criminals cannot be rehabilitated. Because these arguments rest on contradicting assumptions about human behavior, the use of capital punishment to deter crime is problematic. In order for the penal system to work effectively, a third alternative to these contradictory theories must be recognized. People must be viewed as being significantly influenced by external factors, such as poverty and abuse, which can result in criminal behavior. Moreover, according to the same theory, criminals can be taught moral responsibility so that they can attain their freedom.

On Friday, March 9, 2001, Lionel Tate, a Black fourteen-year-old Florida boy, was sentenced to life in prison without parole—for a crime he committed when he was twelve. This life sentence rests upon the assumption that, at twelve, Lionel Tate was fully responsible for the killing of Tiffany Eunick, age six. In addition, the sentence appears to presume that at no time in the long life remaining to him can this child be rehabilitated. He freely chose to do what he did, we are told, and now "He must pay for it."

The same defenders of the criminal justice status quo assure us that sentences such as these deter similar crimes. This opinion is shared by defenders of capital punishment. While insisting that the death penalty deters murder, they would have us believe at the same time that convicted killers are beyond redemption—that all attempts to rehabilitate them will fail.

Few proponents of this theory of justice seem to be aware that it rests upon two fundamentally contradictory views of human nature: it is both *deterministic* (in holding that punishment can *cause* others to be deterred from crime) and *indeterministic* (in proclaiming that incarceration *cannot cause* the culprit to be rehabilitated). This incoherent view of human nature reflects a larger inconsistency that is manifested in the extant politics and corporate practices of our day. One face of this contradiction, which we will call "the operative theory," is presupposed in marketing strategies and political campaigns. The other face, "the public theory," is encountered in political rhetoric and corporate public relations campaigns.

The operative theory

By this account, human motives can be identified, mapped, and measured, and, when applied to a marketing or a political campaign, this knowledge can be put to effective use. (Lately, the strategies and tactics of advertisers and politicians have become virtually identical, as the same "experts" manage both marketing and political campaigns). If public tastes and opinions do not incline toward the company's product or the party's candidate, then these tastes can be "manufactured" to order.

Evidence? Consider annual expenditures for advertising—more than $30 billion just for television ads. Business enterprises will not casually throw that kind of cash at the television industry without a firm and proven expectation that such investments will produce the intended results, namely sales. As [journalist] Vance Packard pointed out a generation ago, and [interviewer] Bill Moyers a decade ago, all the accumulated skills and knowledge of behavioral science are put to use to the task of utilizing, and perchance creating, public motives and tastes to profitable ends. No laboratory of applied psychology is more lavishly funded than that of the market researcher. From Dr. Ernest Dichter's application of Freudian "depth psychology" in the 1930s to GOP pollster Frank Luntz's "focus group" microanalyses in the 2000 presidential campaign, "the consumer and citizen mind" is examined, cross-examined, and meticulously inventoried, and this information is then applied to the greater benefit of the candidate or the bottom line.

> *While insisting that the death penalty deters murder, [capital punishment advocates] would have us believe at the same time that convicted killers are beyond redemption.*

In the jargon of philosophy, the operative theory of marketing and politics is deterministic: that is, it holds that human behavior ("output") is the result of prior experiences ("input"), and that if the inputs are carefully designed and skillfully manipulated, then public motives, tastes, and behavior can be "usefully directed" and even manufactured. Of course, public relations is not an exact science; however, it is a highly empirical and experimental science. Numerous strategies and devices are tried until the public "hot button" is located, whereupon it is "pushed" as long as it "works out." ("Let's run it up the flagpole and see if anyone salutes.") But while there is much trial and error in marketing and political strategies, implicit throughout is the assumption that public behavior is the result of external causes. What then remains is the task of finding and applying the most "efficacious" causes.

The public theory

Corporate spokesmen and their political fellow-travelers (the so-called conservatives) have prepared a contrary theory for public consumption. According to this account, each human personality appears *ex nihilo*, independent, autonomous, and undetermined. Being "unformed" by outside causes, each individual is fully and completely responsible for his or her behavior. "But why does poverty correlate with crime?" No explanation is offered or even felt to be necessary. To cite a typical example, when a conservative lawyer was recently asked on a television talk show why the Columbine High School killers did what they did, her reply was, "Those boys were just evil, that's all." Why they were "evil" was regarded as a pointless question.

[Capital punishment advocates] move back and forth between . . . contradictory . . . theories [of human behavior], as the requirements of public relations and the bottom line demand.

Behavior isn't "caused," this theory asserts, it is simply freely "chosen," and that is all there is to it. "Don't ask me, or 'society,' or (heaven forbid!) the government to do anything about it. It's just not my concern." Clearly, according to this public theory, the only appropriate response to those who commit crimes is "lock 'em up." If the culprits are given less than a life sentence, then we can only hope for the best when they are released. No point in attempting rehabilitation or teaching a useful skill to prepare them for life after release.

As with behavior, so too with public taste and preferences. Tobacco companies tell us that "We are only giving the public what it wants." Likewise, from the media we hear, "Don't complain to us about the sex, violence, and vulgarity in the movies, on television, or in rock lyrics. We're only giving the public what it wants." Those "wants," we are told, which free enterprising entrepreneurs are so generously satisfying, also appear *ex nihilo*—uncaused and freely chosen by each consumer-citizen. "What the public wants" is thus unexplained and unexplainable, and thus out of reach of "cultivation." It follows that there is no need to squander tax money on art and music education, or on noncommercial public broadcasting.

According to the public theory, marketing has no side effects or unintended consequences. Sex-saturated ads and media are totally disconnected from the incidence of teen pregnancy and single-parent families.

"Just do it!" say the ads. "Just say no!" reply the Christian conservatives. But if the teens "do it" anyway, don't blame the promoters. The kids are "just sinful." A child's encounter with tens of thousands of depictions of violent murders on television, we are expected to believe, has nothing to do with whatever violent behavior he or she might exhibit. "Guns (and the gun culture) don't kill people, (autonomous) people kill people."

In sum, the public theory insists that "private enterprise" bears no responsibility whatever for social problems. "The social responsibility of business," [political commentator] Milton Friedman once wrote, "is to increase its profits." All social problems, according to this theory, issue from the uncaused and freely chosen behavior of "simply evil" individuals.

The contradiction

It is abundantly clear that these two "theories" are radically contradictory. If business executives genuinely believed the nondeterminist theory that they present to the public, they would not invest a thin dime in their advertising campaigns. On the other hand, if they were to extend the determinist operative theory beyond their corporate conduct, they would be burdened with a responsibility for the harmful "side effects" of their marketing schemes—effects upon public health, taste, and morality. Instead, they move back and forth between these contradictory determinist and indeterminist theories, as the requirements of public relations and the bottom line demand—all with the ease with which one sheds one's raincoat and puts on one's sunglasses as the weather changes.

In the same way, when conservatives claim (contra the evidence) that capital punishment deters murder, they are determinist. But when they refuse to attempt to rehabilitate incarcerated prisoners, preferring "retribution" and "punishment," they are indeterminists again. According to this latter view, because convicted murderers are "beyond redemption," the only suitable response to their crimes is to "do away with them."

There is a third alternative to these contradictory theories—what philosophers call "compatibilism." By this account, human beings are significantly influenced by the circumstances of their birth and upbringing, and thus criminals are more likely to emerge from conditions of poverty and abuse. However, unless severely traumatized by such misfortunes, most individuals can be educated to a condition of moral responsibility—informed as to the consequences of their acts, recognizing the humanity and dignity of others, and capable of acting according to moral principles—whereupon each attains the freedom to conduct his or her own life.

This is the humane theory and practice of penology found in most enlightened nations. Sadly, the United States of America has yet to achieve this stage of civilization.

Organizations to Contact

The editors have compiled the following list of organizations concerned with the issues debated in this book. The descriptions are derived from materials provided by the organizations. All have publications or information available for interested readers. The list was compiled on the date of publication of the present volume; the information provided here may change. Be aware that many organizations take several weeks or longer to respond to inquiries, so allow as much time as possible.

Amnesty International USA (AI)
322 Eighth Ave., New York, NY 10001
(212) 807-8400 • fax: (212) 627-1451
website: www.amnesty-usa.org

AI is an independent worldwide movement working impartially for the release of all prisoners of conscience, fair and prompt trials for political prisoners, and an end to torture and executions. AI is funded by donations from its members and supporters throughout the world. AI has published several books and reports, including *Fatal Flaws: Innocence and the Death Penalty*.

Canadian Coalition Against the Death Penalty (CCADP)
PO Box 38104, 550 Eglinton Ave. W, Toronto, ON M5N 3A8 CANADA
(416) 693-9112 • fax: (416) 686-1630
e-mail: ccadp@home.com • website: www.ccadp.org

CCADP is a not-for-profit international human rights organization dedicated to educating on alternatives to the death penalty worldwide and to providing emotional and practical support to death row inmates, their families, and the families of murder victims. The center releases pamphlets and periodic press releases, and its website includes a student resource center providing research information on capital punishment.

Capital Punishment Project
American Civil Liberties Union (ACLU)
125 Broad St., 18th Fl., New York, NY 10004
(212) 549-2500 • fax: (212) 549-2646
website: www.aclu.org

The project is dedicated to abolishing the death penalty. The ACLU believes that capital punishment violates the Constitution's ban on cruel and unusual punishment as well as the requirements of due process and equal protection under the law. It publishes and distributes numerous books and pamphlets, including *The Case Against the Death Penalty* and *Frequently Asked Questions Concerning the Writ of Habeas Corpus and the Death Penalty*.

Death Penalty Focus of California
870 Market St., Suite 859, San Francisco, CA 94102
(415) 243-0143 • fax: (415) 243-0994
e-mail: info@deathpenalty.org • website: www.deathpenalty.org

Death Penalty Focus of California is a nonprofit organization dedicated to the abolition of capital punishment through grassroots organizations, research, and the dissemination of information about the death penalty and its alternatives. It publishes the quarterly newsletter *The Sentry*.

Death Penalty Information Center (DPIC)
1320 18th St. NW, 2nd Fl., Washington, DC 20036
(202) 293-6970 • fax: (202) 822-4787
e-mail: pbernstein@deathpenaltyinfo.org • website: www.deathpenaltyinfo.org

DPIC conducts research into public opinion on the death penalty. The center believes that capital punishment is discriminatory and excessively costly and that it may result in the execution of innocent persons. The center publishes numerous reports, such as *Millions Misspent: What Politicians Don't Say About the High Costs of the Death Penalty, Innocence and the Death Penalty: Assessing the Danger of Mistaken Executions,* and *With Justice for Few: The Growing Crisis in Death Penalty Representation.*

Justice Fellowship (JF)
PO Box 16069, Washington, DC 20041-6069
(703) 904-7312 • fax: (703) 478-9679
website: www.justicefellowship.org

This Christian organization bases its work for reform of the justice system on the concept of victim-offender reconciliation. It does not take a position on the death penalty, but it publishes the pamphlet *Capital Punishment: A Call to Dialogue.*

Justice for All (JFA)
PO Box 55159, Houston, TX 77255
(713) 935-9300 • fax: (713) 935-9301
e-mail: info@jfa.net • website: www.jfa.net

JFA is a not-for-profit criminal justice reform organization that supports the death penalty. Its activities include circulating online petitions to keep violent offenders from being paroled early and publishing the monthly newsletter *The Voice of Justice.*

Lamp of Hope Project
PO Box 305, League City, TX 77574-0305
e-mail: aspanhel@airmail.net • website: www.lampofhope.org

The project was established and is run primarily by Texas death row inmates. It works for victim-offender reconciliation and for the protection of the civil rights of prisoners, particularly the right of habeas corpus appeal. It publishes and distributes the periodic *Texas Death Row Journal.*

Lincoln Institute for Research and Education
1001 Connecticut Ave. NW, Suite 1135, Washington, DC 20036
(202) 223-5112

The institute is a conservative think tank that studies public policy issues affecting the lives of black Americans, including the issue of the death penalty, which it favors. It publishes the quarterly *Lincoln Review.*

National Coalition to Abolish the Death Penalty (NCADP)
1436 U St. NW, Suite 104, Washington, DC 20009
(202) 387-3890 • fax: (202) 387-5590
e-mail: info@ncadp.org • website: www.ncadp.org

NCADP is a collection of more than 115 groups working together to stop executions in the United States. The organization compiles statistics on the death penalty. To further its goal, the coalition publishes *Legislative Action to Abolish the Death Penalty*, information packets, pamphlets, and research materials.

National Criminal Justice Reference Service (NCJRS)
U.S. Department of Justice
PO Box 6000, Rockville, MD 20849-6000
(301) 519-5500 • (800) 851-3420
e-mail: askncjrs@ncjrs.org • website: www.ncjrs.org

NCJRS is one of the most extensive sources of information on criminal and juvenile justice in the world. For a nominal fee, this clearinghouse provides topical searches and reading lists on many areas of criminal justice, including the death penalty. It publishes an annual report on capital punishment.

Bibliography

Books

| James R. Acker, Robert M. Bohm, and Charles S. Lanier, eds. | *America's Experiment with Capital Punishment: Reflections on the Past, Present, and Future of the Ultimate Penal Sanction.* Durham, NC: Carolina Academic Press, 1998. |

Stuart Banner — *The Death Penalty: An American History.* Boston: Harvard University Press, 2002.

Hugo Adam Bedau, ed. — *The Death Penalty in America: Current Controversies.* New York: Oxford University Press, 1997.

Corey Lang Brettschneider — *Punishment, Property and Justice.* Burlington, VT: Ashgate, 2001.

Mark Costanzo — *Just Revenge: Costs and Consequences of the Death Penalty.* New York: St. Martin's Press, 1997.

Raphael Goldman — *Capital Punishment.* Washington, DC: CQ Press, 2002.

Harry Henderson — *Capital Punishment.* New York: Facts On File, 2000.

Jesse L. Jackson Sr., Jesse L. Jackson Jr., and Bruce Shapiro — *Legal Lynching: The Death Penalty and America's Future.* New York: New Press, 2001.

Michael A. Mello and David Von Drehle — *Dead Wrong: A Death Row Penalty Lawyer Speaks Out Against Capital Punishment.* Madison: University of Wisconsin Press, 1998.

Greg Mitchell and Robert J. Lifton — *Who Owns Death?: Capital Punishment, the American Conscience, and the End of Executions.* New York: William Morrow, 2000.

Stephen Nathanson — *An Eye for an Eye: The Immorality of Punishing by Death.* Lanham, MD: Rowman & Littlefield, 2001.

Lane Nelson and Burk Foster — *Death Watch: A Death Penalty Anthology.* Upper Saddle River, NJ: Prentice-Hall, 2000.

Louis P. Pojman and Jeffrey Reiman — *The Death Penalty: For and Against.* Lanham, MD: Rowman & Littlefield, 1998.

Austin Sarat — *When the State Kills: Capital Punishment and the American Condition.* Princeton, NJ: Princeton University Press, 2001.

Lloyd Steffen — *Executing Justice: The Moral Meaning of the Death Penalty.* Cleveland, OH: Pilgrim Press, 1998.

Periodicals

Frank Green — "Rethinking the Death Penalty; Terrorism May Have Altered Public Sentiment," *Richmond Times-Dispatch*, October 1, 2001.

Marvin Kitman — "The Reality of Must-Kill TV; If Executions Deter Crime, Why Not Show Them Live?" *Newsday*, May 9, 2001.

Roger Mahony — "Defend Life by Taking It?" *Sojourners*, September/October 2000.

Mike Males — "Percentage Issue," *OC Weekly*, December 10, 1999.

Iain Murray — "More Executions, Fewer Deaths?" *American Outlook*, Fall 2001.

Sean O'Malley — "The Gospel of Life vs. the Death Penalty, *Origins*, April 1, 1999.

Ernest Partridge — "The Two Faces of Justice," *Free Inquiry*, Summer 2001.

Sandra Schneider — "The Goal of Public Humiliation Is Protection of Status Quo," *National Catholic Reporter*, August 27, 1999.

Michelangelo Signorile — "Killing the 20th Hijacker," *New York Press*, April 4, 2002.

Joseph Sobran — "The Best Case Against the Death Penalty," *Conservative Chronicle*, October 11, 2000.

Jessica Stern — "Execute Terrorists at Our Own Risk," *New York Times*, February 28, 2001.

Richard Taylor — "Getting Tough on Crime," *Free Inquiry*, Summer 2001.

Stuart Taylor Jr. — "Does the Death Penalty Save Innocent Lives?" *National Journal*, May 26, 2001.

William Tucker — "Why the Death Penalty Works; The News Will Kill Opponents of Capital Punishment, but Murder Rates Go Down When Execution Numbers Go Up," *American Spectator*, October 1, 2000.

Ernest van den Haag — "The Ultimate Penalty . . . and a Just One: The Basics of Capital Punishment, *National Review*, June 11, 2001.

Index

African Americans
  criminal justice system as harsher to, 17
  death penalty for, 43–44
  murder rate–death penalty correlation and, 11–12
Alaska, 11, 15
American Civil Liberties Union (ACLU), 10
American Society of Criminology (ASC), 61
Anderson, Judith A., 47
Aquinas, Thomas, 31
Arizona, 60
Ashcroft, John, 6, 42, 45, 46

Barnes, Clifford, 51
Bedau, Hugo Adam, 8
Blackmun, Harry, 44
Bonner, Raymond, 14
born-again faith, 40–41
Bowers, William J., 8, 33, 34
Brasfield, Philip, 39
Brennan, William, 25
brutalization theory
  lack of evidence for, 27
  strong evidence for, 8, 32–35, 60–61
Bryjak, George J., 42
Bush, George W., 41

California
  brutalization effect in, 61
  death penalty costs in, 55
Camus, Albert, 30
Carlisle, Peter, 16
Carneal, Michael, 37
children. See juveniles
"compatibilism," 66
Connecticut, 12, 17
convicts. See criminals; prison inmates
Costanzo, Mark, 32
crimes
  coordinated with punishment, 21–22
criminals
  as influenced by external factors, 64–65, 66
  lack of calculation by, 29–30
  root of criminality of, 28–29
  social responsibility of, 65, 66
  see also murder; prison inmates

Dahmer, Jeffrey L., 17–18
death penalty
  arguments against, 14–15, 30–31
  arguments for, 15, 42
  cost of, 30, 54–55
    diverts money from other crime control, 55–56
    negatively impacts criminal justice agencies, 56
    reasons for high, 56–57
  deterrent effect of, is not effective, 16–17
  as encouraging murder, 8, 27, 32–35, 60–61
  finality of, 29
  and innocent people, 34–35
  is not justified, 17–18
  for juveniles, 36, 38, 41
  legal cases with, vs. cases without, 16
  life imprisonment as alternative to, 19–20
  for minorities, 18
  sanctity of life and, 25
  scientific research on, 53–54
  state efforts to reinstate, 15–16, 19
  for terrorist attacks, 6
  as worst kind of crime-control policy, 61–62
  see also public execution(s)
death row inmates
  juvenile, 36–37
  race of, 43–44
  white victims of, 17
  see also prison inmates
Deffered, Ray Martin, 37
deterrence effect
  arguments for, 26
  calculation by criminals and, 29–30
  contradictory views on human nature for, 63–66
  death penalty is not effective for, 16–17
  debate on, 6, 7–8
  defined, 7
  as justifiable, 22
  lack of evidence for, 14, 15, 57–60
  murder rate is affected by, 6–7, 9–13
  public executions and, 32–33, 42–44, 47–48
  rationality for, 35
  as saving lives, 25–26, 28

72